Only Human:

A Journey from Convict to Mentor

By Alton Lane

with Meghan Vigeant

Belfast, ME   2016

Printed by Create Space
Layout by Merlin Design, Blue Hill, ME
Photos by David Smith
Cover by accent design, Alna, ME

Contents

PART II

Preface

This narrative was crafted by personal historian Meghan Vigeant (www.storiestotell.net) based on interviews with Alton Lane in 2015. The material has been edited and arranged for narrative effect and clarity, but every effort has been made to maintain Alton's intentions and voice.

Note from the Author

Some names and identifying details have been changed to protect the privacy of individuals. I have tried to recreate events, locales and conversations from my memory. In order to maintain their anonymity, in some instances, I have changed the names of individuals and places. I have also changed some identifying characteristics and details such as physical properties, occupations and places of residence.

Introduction

When I was a boy I'd wake up in the morning to the sound of the birds chirping. They sounded so happy. I'd take my BB gun, go outside, and try to shoot the birds. I hated birds. I hated happy people. Happy people pissed me off more than anything in my life, because I couldn't be happy. It made me sad to hear birds singing about their happiness, knowing that I could never be. I'll never be happy. How can I? I'm a pretty strange feller. How can I ever be happy? That's what was going on in my mind.

Today, I have such a different outlook on life that I don't recognize myself sometimes. I can actually say, "I'm happy" and mean it. I wake up with a smile on my face instead of kicking the dog. I drink my coffee in the morning, look out the window and watch the birds. I put feed out for the birds; they eat better than I do. I enjoy watching them. When I see a bird looking at me through the window, I wonder, What is that bird thinking? What's going on in that little fellow's head? It's cool to be able to look outside yourself at someone else, like the birds, and see their day-to-day lives.

My thoughts are so different from what they used to be. Sometimes I can't even believe I can say, "I love myself. I'm a good person." That sounds almost like gibberish to me. I start asking myself, "Who are you? Oh yeah. I forgot. That's me!" It's such a difference from the way I saw myself before: "I hate you. Why don't you just die?" It stings to hear those words. Now, it's cool to be able to walk around with my head up, a smile on my face. To know that I'm willing to give everything I have to help another person, everything I have. If there could be a few more people in the world that came to this understanding – we could make this a beautiful place. We could make this a peaceful place.

"Non-violence means avoiding not only external physical violence but also internal violence of spirit. You not only refuse to shoot a man, but you refuse to hate him." - Martin Luther King, Jr.

When I heard people talking about Martin Luther King, Jr. I used to say, "That guy's an idiot. He's a moron. He don't know what the hell he's talking about. What a happy-go-lucky dumb ass." Now I hold his words very dear. I have great respect for people with that kind of courage. I hope some day I can have that kind of courage. I guess in some ways I already do.

I guess really what I'm trying to say is – I discovered that by changing the way I think I really could change my behavior. I know I couldn't have done it overnight. Change happened one little small piece at a time. Eventually I noticed those little changes in my life made up a bigger change. That's how it happened.

This book is the story of my life of violence, both kinds — physical violence and the internal violence of the mind. It's also about how I learned another way, one of nonviolent thought, communication and compassion. Now I'm the one who sounds like a happy-go-lucky dumb ass, eh? Well, maybe I am, but it doesn't bother me if you think that, not anymore. I'm happy to be me. Here's the story, a long journey of how I finally found happiness within.

PART

I

Violence Makes the World Go Round

I was never a stranger to violence. Right from an early age, I knew violence made the world go round.

My earliest memory: I was three-years-old. I remember playing outside and hearing yelling and things smashing in my aunt and uncle's trailer next door. We knew my aunt would be coming over soon with black eyes. Many times she showed up at our trailer door with her face half beat in, asking my father to protect her. Once my father punched his own brother out to get him to stop beating her. I've seen her face so swollen it was purple. One time he tried to drown her in a pot of lobster water. Her face was all scarred with big blisters. You almost couldn't tell she had lips. She still has wrinkles in her face today from it.

I saw a lot of stuff like that as a kid and never really gave it a second thought. I thought it was okay. I was taught, "you make your own bed." That's what I told myself to justify the whole thing. If she didn't want this to happen, she'd stop doing what she's doing. My uncle spent over half his life in prison from the beatings he gave his wife and her lovers.

Let's just clear one thing up. My father was an abuser too. After I was born he quit drinking so I didn't see as much physical violence from him while I was growing up. But he still had it in him. My father was a man of very few words.

He only told you once. If you didn't get his point, you'd get it right up side the head. It was just a common part of life, and we knew it.

Even other people would beat my ass when I misbehaved, even at bible meetings. Later at home, my parents would tell me, "You're an embarrassment. I'm gonna kick your ass," and they would. My mother beat my ass with a wooden spoon. "You will learn. Especially when we're at other people's houses." That was the worst. I didn't even like going to other people's houses. I had to sit there like a statue. I had to wait for them to get done. If I was good I might get a milkshake from McDonalds.

I always promised myself I would never be an abuser. That's not gonna be me. I'm gonna be the first person in this family that's not like that. It wasn't too many years later I found out that's just what I was. Violence was second nature to me.

When I was about five years old I got to be friends with a kid from my neighborhood, Mark, a little skinny fellow in the first grade with really thick glasses. The fourth graders used to pick on him a lot. I was only in kindergarten, but I was a pretty good-sized kid, as big as any fourth grader. One day Mark asked me if I'd be his bodyguard. He said he'd let me drive his father's lawn tractor anytime. Whenever they started picking on Mark, I'd beat the hell out of those fourth graders. They left him alone after about three beatings. I thought it was pretty cool these older kids were afraid of me. Plus, I got to ride his tractor.

Secret

When I was five years old my mother started leaving me with a babysitter when she went to work as a waitress. The sitter had a 17-year-old son. He was a weird kid. Sometimes he shit his own pants. One day, mom left me during a vacation day when he was home from school. We were both outside. He was building a shed next to their house. I turned around and there was his penis in my face. I wanted to throw up. My stomach turned. I wanted to cry. I thought I was doing something wrong. That was the first time.

Then, anytime we were alone, he'd do something to me. He didn't care where we were. He did stuff to me in Reny's parking lot waiting for his mother to come out of the store. When he graduated from school the next year he was always at home. It didn't stop, and I was afraid. This went on for seven years.

I thought something was wrong with me. I remember feeling dirty. It was a feeling I couldn't shake, a feeling of worthlessness. I just hoped nobody ever found out. I couldn't tell my parents. I worried that my father might think I was gay, or that my father might kill him and go to prison and then I wouldn't have a father. I didn't know what to do, so I bit my tongue and kept it to myself. After this started happening I didn't want to spend time with my parents any more. I worried they might know something was wrong with me. From then on, my relationship with my parents went downhill. It was my choice. I was just a scared little kid.

Hellfire and Brimstone

One Sunday, I was sitting in church with my family and my mother went up to the front. There were three guys up there. They all put this oil on their hands and then put their hands on my mother's head and started saying something like, "haka waka waka." My mother dropped to the floor with a crash. She was knocked right out, unconscious. I tried to run up to her, but my dad came up and grabbed me. "You sit down and shut up." That scared the shit out of me. One minute my mother was standing; next minute she's unconscious. I was seven years old the first time I saw my mother "slain in the spirit," as they call it.

After that incident I sat underneath my seat a lot. I didn't want to be part of it. I didn't want to see it. I didn't want to hear it. I didn't want any of it. I thought it was crazy. Just insane. There were always people bouncing, jumping up and down, and rolling in the aisle talking weird. It sounded like different languages. It was freaky. All they talked about was how awesome Jesus Christ is and his unending love and power.

I was glad when I was finally old enough to take off and do what I wanted. Sundays, I'd get up first thing in the morning, take off to a friend's house or ride my bike. I'd even go sit in the woods. I really didn't care what, just anything but that.

I grew up in a strict religious home. Because my parents belonged to a Pentecostal church there were a lot of things us kids weren't allowed to do. We couldn't dress up in costumes and go trick or treating at Halloween. I couldn't even watch the kids' show The Smurfs because the characters Gargamel and his cat Azrael are names of demons in the Bible.[1] Dad only watched the news and Hee-Haw. Sometimes if Dad was working and Mom wasn't paying attention you could slip in a few minutes of TV and nobody would know. As a kid, it really sucked.

I was the youngest of six kids. Most of my siblings were out of the house by the time I came around. My sister Dawn lived with us till she was sixteen. She was the rebellious one. I remember when she started disappearing during church time. We lived in an apartment directly above the church. You could go through the Sunday school room, walk up the stairs into our bathroom and into our apartment. Dawn would tell Mom, "I've got to go to the bathroom," and she'd go upstairs and not come back until a few minutes before church was over.

One day I thought I'd check out what Dawn was up to. I said to Mom, "I got to go to the bathroom." I went upstairs and there's my sister Dawn watching American Bandstand on TV. "Oooh! I love American Bandstand." I sat down with her to watch. Probably five minutes before church was over, my mother's head popped through the bathroom door. She was pissed. She almost killed us both. "It's church time and you two are up here watching rock n' roll music!" The wooden spoon came out. "I'm gonna tell your father."

---

1   While Azarael does appear in religious texts, sometimes as a fallen angel of death, Gargamel does not appear in the bible. During the 80's some Christians viewed the Smurfs as a show that promoted witchcraft and saw it as inappropriate for children.

"Don't tell Dad," I said. "I'll beat myself."

By this time in my life, I was running the streets. I could create my own hellfire and brimstone. One day, I pulled every fire alarm on all the telephone poles that I could put my hands on. The police chief was pissed but I didn't go to jail because I was only seven. My young age didn't stop me from making trouble though.

I used to steal my mother's cigarettes and my friend Hal and I would hide out in the bamboo and smoke cigarettes.

Then there was the time I set a fire at the Belfast Variety Store. I was hanging out with my cousin and only had three matches. I said, "Let's go to the store and get some matches." So we walked across the street to the store.

I said to the woman behind the counter, "Look man, I need some matches."

She said, "I'm not giving you matches. What are you stupid?"

At this, I went outside and used one of my three matches to light a cigarette and threw the lit match in the trashcan. Then I lit my other two matches and threw those in the trashcan too. A four-foot flame billowed out of the trashcan, right next to the gas pump. I screamed to no one in particular, "I'll blow everyone of you up. You give me some matches!"

There was a slow burn going on inside me, red hot. I didn't know how to cool my anger. Something was bound to catch fire.

Throwing Wood With My Father

My father, Beverly Lane, was a big man, one of the strongest men I've ever known. He weighed a solid 240 pounds, kind of like the trunk of a tree. He was almost six-feet tall, just massive. A man of very few words. When he did speak, he used a commanding and stern voice. If he told you to shut up, you felt it deep inside, tingly.

He had only three interests in life: church, work, and watching the news. That's all he really had time for. He'd work from the first thing in the morning till dark. Dad was big on quiet too. He didn't like a lot of horsing around. When he was home from work, better shut your mouth. Be quiet. There wasn't a lot of time for playing baseball or going fishing or, "Hey boy, how you doing?" None of that.

Mostly, I spent time with Dad working in the woods. That was our father and son time. He cut pulp wood most of his life. I can remember him putting me up in the seat of the tractor when I was about four years old and walking beside me while I drove. He bought me a little chainsaw, a Stihl, and taught me how to use it. My mother didn't like the idea of me having a saw. I thought it was great.

I started working with him in the woods right from five or six years old. I'd walk through the woods after he cut the trees down and drag these four-foot pieces of wood and put them in a pile. The big ones, of course, he had to handle. But for the most part I was a pretty rugged kid at an early age.

Our day usually started at five o'clock in the morning. We'd drive to the wood lot while it was still dark out. By the time the sky lightened up we were walking in the woods getting ready. My father would cut fir and spruce trees down, trim the limbs off, and cut the tree into four-foot pieces.

My father could eyeball a tree and tell you within a foot where that tree was going to land. He'd make a notch in the front where he wanted the tree to fall. He'd take a little slice out like a piece of pie, back cut, and the tree would fall right where he said it would. If you weren't paying attention, he could make a tree come down, snap, and whip the top of the tree across your back. He liked doing that to me. He thought that was funny. I would be taking a break over by the water jug. (He didn't like taking breaks much, so he'd send a tree my way.) I'd jump. "What the hell is that?" But after a while, I learned. I just didn't turn my back to him.

Uncle Danny cut wood with my father quite a bit. He'd get out of the truck and leave behind a half chewed cigar, still smoking in the ashtray. He'd say to me, "Alright, take this out to your father and hurry up." I'd get in the jitterbug and start chewing and smacking and puffing away on that old cigar as I drove through the woods.

One day I got in the truck with Dad at the wheel and Uncle Danny in the passenger seat. We'd been cutting wood on the Bangor-Veazie line, right by the Orono dump. The ground was a little wet, and we were bouncing over mud holes on the way out of the woods. I pulled one of Uncle Danny's chewed-up cigar butts out of my pocket and grabbed the lighter from the ashtray. My father looked at me like: what the hell do you think you're doing? He ripped that cigar butt right out of my mouth and threw it out the window. He had a few choice words for me too. Boy, was he mad.

We lost that land after my aunt and uncles decided they weren't interested in paying any money towards the taxes. So the town actually took the land. It was 75 acres. They called it Lot 17. Ironically, my dad and uncle started cutting wood to pay the tax bill.

I really liked working with Dad in the wintertime because he would light a fire when the chainsaw ran out of gas. He'd fill the saw up with gas and we'd stand around the fire for a minute. He'd always bring a package of hot dogs for lunch. We could actually stop and take a break for lunch. There weren't a lot of breaks with Dad. We only stopped long enough to eat our lunch and get back to work.

I think that's where I get my work ethic today. I work all day and all evening. I lift stuff that really three people ought to lift. I guess that's one thing I learned from my dad: how to be a survivor. Doesn't matter if you like what you're doing or not, as long as you're earning a paycheck, making a living, supporting your family.

I still cut wood sometimes. Somebody'll call me up, "Want to cut some wood?" But cutting wood now is different. Back then you could make enough money to survive. Now it's really hard unless you have the machinery, the skidders, and the log trucks. I do it now just for a little extra cash. When I'm out there the smells really bring me back to those days in the woods with Dad, like when I'm limbing a spruce tree. Dad used to bring home spruce gum. It's a sap old-timers used to cut off and chew. Last time I was cutting wood I brought some home for my sister, a whole branch full of it. She hadn't had it in 20 years. She was excited. I love the smell of a wood yard, especially cutting fir, spruce, pine. There's just something settling about it.

I remember I liked driving the jitterbug in the woods the most. It was a time when I got to be alone and I could actually be a kid when nobody was looking. I ran over trees and stumps and beat through the mud holes. It was just fun. I could drive into a tree on accident and just back up and keep going. It was like breaking a rule. Ha ha! I got away with it.

The jitterbug was a 1949 Dodge army truck, six by six, and full of quirks. The key to the ignition broke and you had to cross the solenoid with a screwdriver to make it start. It was so low geared you could get out of it while it was in motion, take a leak, and get back in again. It wouldn't have gone very far. It was just that slow.

My uncle started the jitterbug one day and forgot to take it out of gear. He was a full-fledged drinker and had already had a 12-pack that morning no problem. The truck started going backwards and one of the chains caught his leg and knocked him down. The jitterbug drove, real slow like, up one leg and came right up his stomach and across his chest, 1,000 pounds weighing on him. He thought it was gonna kill him. He saw that tire coming for his face and he twisted his head as much as he could. He was lucky. My father got there and saw the jitterbug going and asked himself, what the hell? The jitterbug's backed up into the woods. Where's Danny? Dad walked over and there's Uncle Danny pushed down into the mud under the truck. Lucky there was mud there. Uncle Danny was scared. Didn't slow him down though. He got right up, went over and grabbed a beer.

Lessons I Learned from a Case of Golden Anniversary

I started working on a cow farm up the road for a few days a week. I'd lug grain and shovel manure. During the summer we'd hay. I earned two dollars a day. But I was a kid, just 10 years old. I worked with three brothers: Buddy, Frank and Ted. At the end of the week, I'd say, "Let's walk to the store. Let's get some beer." The oldest, would just tell me to beat it. Buddy wasn't old enough to buy it. But Frank, he'd be up for it.

Frank was 22 years old so he could legally buy alcohol, but he was mentally challenged. He could barely spell his own name. Even though he was older, we were about the same mentality. He was my man. We'd walk down to the store and get beer and cigarettes. We usually got this stuff called Golden Anniversary. It was like $2.99 a twelve-pack. It was cheap and nasty. We drank in Frank's camper.

Sometimes we'd go to my house and I'd tell my old man I was going to have a camp out in the woodshed. There was a table and a wood stove out there. So we'd go out there and fire up the wood stove, lock the doors, get hammered, and smoke cigarettes.

That's what we did. Work all week, then take a day and get some beer – pretty rewarding at the end of the week for a young fella. That's how I learned alcohol every day could make life easier for me. I felt better when I drank. It took me away from it all.

One time this woman was jogging down the road and Frank asked her a question, I can't remember what. She was snobby about it. She said, "You guys go fuck yourself. Whatever." I remembered I had this semi-automatic pellet gun that my dad got me. Like a bonehead, I brought that to the farm with me two days later. I'd had three or four beers, which was a good buzz for me at 10. We saw her jog past the farm about 50 or 60 feet away. We shot her in the ass. She started running faster so we hit her four or five times. She ran home. We thought it was funny.

Later when I was staggering home along the road. The cops pulled me over, asked me what I was doing.

"I'm just going home."

"What's in the bag?"

"Nothing. Just going home."

"Let me see your backpack."

"I'm just going home."

They took my backpack and found the pellet gun in it.

The woman had gone home to her husband after we shot her. She had red welts on her back. The husband was going to come down and try to beat us up, but there's not much you can do against a retarded guy and a kid. Makes you look kind of stupid. So they called the cops. She didn't press charges, but she wanted me to know what we did was unacceptable.

That's what it was like with Frank. We just didn't care. Get some beer and life's good. He taught me that alcohol covers up a lot of stuff. It was a lesson that lasted decades. When I'd drink or get high all that stuff sort of went away. I didn't feel it. I didn't even think about it. For the most part, my unhappiness went away, until the next day or the day after that, whenever I sobered up, and then it would be back, even worse.

The Last Time

My father got a job as a mechanical insulator and so we moved to Searsport at the end of my sixth-grade year. While my parents were moving into our new trailer my mother left me with the sitter again, and I didn't have the heart to tell her what he was doing to me. She dropped me off and of course the sitter's son did what he always did to me.

I had enough. I asked the sitter, "Can I use that phone?" I told my mother over the phone, "Look, I don't know what you guys are doing. I don't really care. I'm walking. If you want to, come pick me up. If you don't, I really don't care. Mom, I'm done with this. I really can't do it. So I'm walking. I don't give a shit if I have to sleep in a dumpster. I'm not staying here another day." That's the last time it ever happened.

She never asked me why I just up and left the babysitter's house like that. My mother wasn't the kind of person to ask a bunch of questions.

By the time I was twelve I was kind of scared of girls. I thought I might have some kind of gay magnet. I kept questioning my sexuality because some dude did what he did. I knew deep down I wasn't gay, but it was pretty obvious there was something wrong with me. I shouldn't have had to go through that at 12 years old. I should have been a normal happy kid.

What's Wrong With You?

During my first week of school at Searsport I walked up the road and these two guys asked me if I wanted to get high. I said, "Yeah! Where the hell have you been?" That's how I met Larry and Bob. Later on in life when I got hooked on heroin and I was too shaky to do it myself, these two guys would stick the needle in for me. So that first week, bang! I didn't even have a chance. My first two friends – we were drinking, partying, and using whatever we could get our hands on every weekend, every day, anytime we could.

These guys didn't know anything about me. They didn't look at me and see something wrong. Getting high and drunk with these guys felt good. Once I got ahold of that feeling it really set in. This is what I need to be accepted. I need to be so messed up I don't even know what I'm saying. So that's what I did.

I didn't feel like I fit in at school, so I became the joker of the class. I would make stupid comments, rude jokes to make everybody laugh. I'd do obnoxious stuff. A lot of times I wouldn't do any work. In seventh grade the other kids were taking computer class and I was skipping. I was out back smoking pot. My teachers passed me just to get rid of me, just to keep me moving. Get out of my class.

I didn't think I was smart like the other kids. I had a hard time learning. I was really behind on math. I didn't want to be the stupid kid asking all the questions. I got sent to the office as much as I could, so I wouldn't embarrass myself. That's the way I thought about it then.

People were afraid of me, even grown people. By third or fourth grade I was beating up middle school guys on the bus. Jumping on their back, putting the knuckles right to their head. I did it numerous times. I just didn't care. Most of those guys were three times the size of me; I'd still put a knuckle right in their ear. It didn't faze me.

One day in science class we were doing a project, taking pictures and articles out of magazines and pasting them onto a piece of paper, a collage or something like that. I told the teacher, "This is stupid. It's not teaching me anything. What's the sense of being here?" She made a really smartass comment (I thought). I took my magazines, opened them all up and stood them up on my desk then I lit them all on fire.

I basically just did it for a way to get out of school, but they wouldn't suspend me anymore. They kept putting me on in-school suspension because I kept doing stuff trying to get suspended. I was really trying to get expelled. I tried to quit school when I was 14 years old. My probation officer told me I couldn't because it was against the law. So I'd show up in homeroom: "I'm here." As soon as the attendance went to the office: "I got to go to the bathroom." I'd leave and meet up with a couple of friends out back and get drunk or high.

Most days I would get out of school and wouldn't even go home. I'd stay at a friend's house for two or three days and we'd party. We drank all the time. My friend's mother was okay with that, as long as we were up in time for school. A lot of times we'd go to school for only a few hours, just to get the attendance and head off and find a jug of vodka. Go relax.

I remember being mean to the other kids. They had more then I ever did and it made me jealous. A friend of mine was telling me all about his snowmobile, this and that. I'm like, "Dude, whatever." He said, "Well, you got nothing, so why would you care?" So I kicked him in the chest and he went right through the glass of the Mott's Apple Juice machine. We weren't friends anymore. The school wanted my mother to buy the machine or pay the $400 to fix it. But we moved away shortly after that happened.

These kids were getting all this really nice stuff. They get to go to their grandparents on the weekends. I never had a grandparent. My grandparents were dead before I was born. My mother's mother disowned us, so she was dead to me anyway. I wished so much that I had what those kids had.

My friends were all pretty much like me – people who had nothing, poor people, no money. We didn't get big presents and all that stuff. We just like to drink and get high and hang around and beat each other up when we're drunk.

My friend Bob, he was the kind of guy who wouldn't piss on a fire to put somebody out. My friend John, Bob's brother, he was more the leader of the group. He was a lot older than I was. He would come up with these ideas of things to do when we were bored. Of course we'd follow him.

One time we were walking around the side streets of Belfast. It was probably 1:30 in the morning. We came up to a Budweiser distributor van. John said, "Dude, I wonder if that's locked up. I wonder if there's any beer in there." So we went over and opened the door. There were five or six kegs in it. We were like, "Oh, my God. Kegs! Woo hoo!" Well, they were all empty. But the front of the van was full of cases of bottled beer. So John went down to the neighbor's, stole their wheelbarrow, and we filled up the wheelbarrow twice. We brought the wheelbarrow back and drank for like three or four days after that.

Probably a month and a half later, we didn't have anything to drink, and John said, "Geez, we ought to go check that van out again." It was probably two o'clock in the morning. The van was there but the doors were locked. We could see cases of beer in it through the dark window. John said, "Well, let's break a window."

I said, "Well, alright! Break a window then. Let's get some beer."

John picked up a rock and threw it at the van and the rock almost hit him bouncing off the window. We're like, "Wow!" We'd never seen that before. So we threw four or five more rocks. Nothing broke. By this time the neighborhood lights started coming on, so we took off. That's the kind of ideas John came up with, the kind of ideas we all followed along with.

Some nights when it was cold we'd sneak into somebody's basement through the bulkhead. We'd just go in, sit down, get warm for a half an hour, and sneak out. Sometimes we'd smoke a joint. There'd be people in the house, but nobody ever came down. Nobody ever heard us. We were pretty quiet. One night we were sitting in somebody's basement during a blizzard. Our friend Rick said, "Man, we can sit in my dad's car and get warm." His father's car didn't need a key. The ignition was broken. So we piled into the car and warmed up. "Jeez, let's go for a ride." So we did. Then John suggested, "There's this little store out in Frankfurt. They got no camera, no security. Let's break in, get some beer and cigarettes." Rick and I were like, "Hey cool. Whatever." We drove through this blizzard to this store. John kicked the door in. We went in and emptied the cooler. The back seat was so full of beer that Rick was practically buried in between cases of beer. We had a box full of cartons of cigarettes.

We headed back to Belfast and were gonna go park the car and party. We got three quarters of the way back to Belfast and John decided to take a dirt road to avoid the cops. We hit a five-foot deep snowdrift and it pulled us right off the road. We blew the back tire trying to get out. So we sat all night in that car. We drank and drank. Ran the car right out of gas.

When I woke up the next morning somebody was knocking on the window. I was hung-over and groggy. I opened up one eye, opened the door, and saw this cop standing there. I shut the door and he knocked again. I nudged John, "Hey, this guy wants to talk to you." I went back to sleep. Obviously, we got arrested.

Most of the time I wasn't thinking about much other than where to get my next high or find booze. That was the main focus in my life. I thought it was great. We're getting hammered. We're getting all fucked up. Nobody could stop us. We thought we had the world by the balls. We didn't care about consequences. By the time I was 14, I told myself I didn't want to live past 25. Twenty-five would be a plenty old age for me. By the time I turned 18 I was already attempting to drink myself to death and doing the biggest pile of drugs I could get my hands on. I just didn't want to live.

There were some people trying to reach out to me. I kept seeing these people over and over as I grew up. In fourth or fifth grade Mrs. Staples started working with me. She was like a traveling guidance counselor. They got me into summer camp one time, thought it would be beneficial, maybe it would get me away from some of my bad behavior.

There was Ms. Becker. She started working with me when I was pretty young, like third grade. She was my first behavior teacher. She was probably the most memorable. She was always positive. She never judged me. She knew I'd screwed up a lot. Even when she was angry she still had this niceness about her. She was cool.

Did any of them make an impact on my behavior or change what I was doing in my life? No. I didn't listen to anybody. I didn't take any kind of criticism, good or bad, especially good criticism. I hated to hear good stuff about myself. When I'd say something like, "I can't do that cause I'm too stupid," a teacher would say, "No, you're smarter than you think." I'd get up and throw a chair across the room. I thought they were just saying that to make me feel better. But as I grew up I realized I am intelligent.

There was this girl in my class named Jennifer. She was the only girl that I really talked with. I was scared of girls. I really was. I felt like girls were actually the smarter species. I believed that after all that shit that happened to me, girls would know something's wrong with me. They'd pick up on that feeling stuff. But I liked talking with Jennifer. She was cool. She was really pretty too. She had strawberry blonde hair. In middle school she was built like a woman. She was a little shorter than me, probably three or four inches shorter than I was. I remember one time they were doing a play in school. Jennifer tried so hard to talk me into doing this stupid play about this jerk of a guy called Master Gloomy or something, I can't even remember. She tried and tried and tried to talk me into doing this play. Finally, I said, "Okay, I'll do it." I played a goblin or a ghoul or something. I went out on stage about three times and just stood there. I didn't have to say anything. It was a little embarrassing standing up there looking stupid in this costume in front of all these people. I wasn't used to that. I didn't even get to dress up in costumes for Halloween because my parents wouldn't let me. I think that was the first and only time I remember my mother coming to the school for something other than a visit to the principal's office.

But Jennifer was nice to me. I guess that's why I talked to her. A lot of the girls weren't. They'd laugh at me. I wouldn't talk to girls. I wouldn't even get near them. I was weird. People were like, "What's wrong with you?"

Crazier Than a Cut Cat

Back then my friends would say I was "crazier than a cut cat." I beat myself with firewood at parties. I broke a frying pan over my head. I put my head through people's walls. I thought I was crazy. Probably half of my friends, if they haven't seen me in 20 years, they'd probably say I'm crazier than hell. Most people never knew the real me.

I didn't know the real me. I knew that life should be a lot different. But I didn't know what was going on inside of me. Anything that resembled a feeling came out as anger. If I was hurt or scared then I lashed out. Every emotion and every feeling went right to insanity.

I used to beat stuff over my head all the time. Usually it was with a stick of firewood, something that could fit in my hands. I'd smash myself in the head with it. Anytime at the end of the night, if I'd been drinking, I'd be angry. A lot of times I did things to keep people away from me. I didn't want people trying to get close, asking me questions. I couldn't let them, couldn't open up that part of me.

One night I was partying at my friend Tina's. I went into Belfast to get some pot and when I got back my friend Bob was in bed with my girlfriend. I was like, "Man, I'm going to fucking kill both of you is what's going to happen." But I left. I went outside. Bob and some other people came outside trying to talk to me. Bob kept saying, "I'm sorry, Alton." So I grabbed up a piece of firewood and started beating myself over the head with it. Everybody was like, "Oh, my god. What the hell are you doing?" They thought I was going to beat Bob with it. It made a lot of people think twice about partying with me. They'd ask me first, "What are you drinking?" or "How much you drink today?" But that was my safety mechanism. People don't want to get close to you when you're like that. It scared Bob right out of his ass. He didn't even dare to come near me for like two weeks. He really thought I was going to kill him.

I remember one time we were arguing because we didn't have any firewood, and I was getting mad. There was this giant penny, about as big around as a bowl and a half-inch thick. I took that and I knotted myself in the head with that like 40 times. I had a bruise that looked like Abraham Lincoln on my forehead. It was ugly. After that people started hiding stuff, anything I might just pick up and hit myself with. Then I got into throwing knives at the floor and stuff. Once, a knife bounced back up, stuck me right in the hand. I didn't do much knife throwing after that.

One day I must have been in the mood for trouble. I was hanging out with my friends. There was a woman we had just met, and we were all sitting around in her apartment in Belfast. We had a half-gallon of vodka each and were chasing it with Colt 45. It was just one of those days. None of us had anything to do. I ran out of cigarettes. Tina had one cigarette left, so we shared that. About 25 minutes later after I drank the last of the vodka. I told them, "This isn't good. I need more vodka and cigarettes." So I said, "I'm going to run downtown and bum a couple cigarettes. I'll be back."

John could see I was really wasted. "Dude, you're not going anywhere." (He probably figured I'd get arrested.) I was 14 years old at the time. The cops had already picked me up a number of times and put me in jail for a couple of days whenever they found me walking around like that.

But I was bullheaded. I told him, "I just got done telling ya. I'm going downtown. I'll be back with some cigarettes."

He insisted, "You're not. You're not going anywhere."

I looked at my friend Tina, "Will you go downtown? See if you can get some cigarettes?"

"Nah, I'm not going anywhere, Alton. I'm hammered."

I said, "Well, alright. Peace out. I'm leaving. See you guys later."

Then John grabbed me and said, "You're not going anywhere."

I grabbed him by his ears and I head-butted his face. I threw him off into a pantry closet. Then I grabbed this woman's pan off her stove, thankfully it wasn't hot, and I started smashing myself in the head with it until I broke the handle off.

I told them, "Anybody comes out, I'll kill every one of ya. Leave me alone." I went out into the hall to try to calm down, but it didn't work.

I knew there was a neighbor in the apartment next door that smoked cigarettes. Knocking on his door, I bellowed, "Somebody's got to have a cigarette." He wouldn't answer his door. "Well, alright then." I took my head and smashed it through his wall right up to my shoulders. There I am, head sticking through the wall over his living room couch, yelling, "I'm gonna goddamn tell ya, I want to have a cigarette!"

His wife shrieked, "What the hell is going on here?" They didn't give me any cigarettes, but they did call the cops. I ran down to the next apartment and threw this woman out of her own apartment. I barricaded myself in her bathroom with a butcher knife. Eventually the cops came in. There were probably 12 cops in that bathroom with me. By the time they got the knife away from me and got me out of the bathroom, they had beat the hell right out of me. I was bleeding all over the place. They arrested me and hauled me out.

My friends laughed at the sight of me, even the friend I had head-butted. I had blood running out of my head all over the place. My white T-shirt, which had a bunch of little devils on it, was all red with blood. Somehow the cops had ripped my pants off in the struggle, and they hauled me out with my long johns halfway down around my ass. My friends thought that was funnier than hell. All I could think about was how I didn't get a cigarette. I was pretty bummed out.

I did 30 days in the county jail. I actually really liked the people at the sheriff's department. I'd go in there for two or three days on a regular basis, and they'd sit with me, watch movies, eat food. It wasn't so bad. My favorite was Ray Porter. He'd bring a whole box of movies. They had a big TV downstairs. He let me watch movies and got me food out of the kitchen. Since I was a juvenile they had to put me down in the basement, separate from the adults. I slept on a cot. I still had to wear one of those stupid orange jumpsuits that were too small. Sometimes there were other kids down there with me. One time my cousin was there. Most of the time it was just the guard and me.

I suppose I did crazy things like smashing my head through walls for the attention. I did it because I was drunk and cocky and would fixate on something unattainable like getting those cigarettes. I didn't really care about the consequences. What are they going to do, I thought, put me in the Youth Center?

Maine Youth Center

At the Maine Youth Center they give you six or seven minutes to wake up and make your bed first thing in the morning. It's like making a bed in the military. You have to be able to bounce a dime off your sheets. Then everybody stands in a line wearing just underwear and a t-shirt waiting to go downstairs for however long the staff wants to make you stand there. Downstairs, you brush your teeth and use the bathroom. But you can't just go ahead and use the bathroom. You have to stand in a line and ask, "Can I use the recess?" And if they say no, you're bummin'. I've seen them do it many, many times.

You'd think somebody would just go in their pants, but most people didn't, because if you did you'd be scrubbing your underwear later that night.

In the evening at shower time everybody stands in line in his underwear. You pull your underwear down and hold it out to show the guy on the laundry crew. If there's anything on your underwear at all, they give you an old toothbrush and you scrub your underwear in the sink. Then you bring it back out and show it to the guy on the laundry crew again. If I was the one sitting there on laundry crew and I felt like being an asshole, I'd be like, " Yeah...that's not good enough. Beat it." I could send them back in there to scrub three times if I felt like it, and then they'd get a write-up. Some of the staff was weird about it. Mr. P– if you wanted to go to the bathroom on his crew, he'd roll the toilet paper out on a school desk and rip it off and give it to you. That's all you got –the size of a school desk. It didn't bother me. I'd just wait until the next staff person came on. Some of them were pretty decent. But there were a lot of stupid things like that. I don't know what the hell they were trying to prove. There were a couple of them that were really mean.

A kid tried to run away once, and a staff member ran to his car and grabbed a golf club. He wound the golf club and took the kid out with it, right out across the back of his head. Took the kid right off his feet.

It was really like a big camp more than anything. We lived in buildings they called cottages. Cottage 1 had people who were being held for court. Cottage 2 was where you got your hair cut. Cottage 3 was for kids in for substance abuse. Cottage 4 was anybody over sixteen. There really wasn't a Cottage 5. Cottage 6 was Hayden; that was for people with mental disabilities. Cottage 7, where I first started, that was for younger people without a lot of substance abuse history. Cottage 8 was the girls' and Cottage 9 was for the sex offenders.

During the day we went to classes. In the summer they might take us outside to play a game of football or whatever. After dinner, we had what they called the reflection hour. You had to write 500 words about anything you'd seen that day. Basically they wanted everybody to rat each other out. Later, there was time to write letters. We didn't really get to watch TV.

It wasn't that bad. I made money while I was there. I worked two jobs in the summer. I worked in the kitchen in the evening and in the laundry during the day. I got paid 75 or 80 bucks a week. I really didn't have to spend much money.

My parents would come every weekend and buy me whatever I needed out of the commissary. So I saved up. When I got out of the Youth Center I had almost 700 bucks. That was pretty cool for a 15-year-old kid. It was quite a party.

There were a lot of childish people in the Youth Center. Half of the kids I was in with, they're sitting in prison right now for years and years. The other half are probably dead from overdosing. You go to prison, and when you get out you still have nothing. Most people go back to the same stuff over and over again. I could easily be in there too, sitting right beside them, doing 20 or 30 years in prison. But somehow, things came out differently for me.

A Working Man

My mother and father didn't have a lot of extra money. We'd go to the Salvation Army and buy new sneakers with holes in them. I told my mother I wanted a new pair of shoes one day. We went into the store and I showed her what I wanted and she laughed at me. "You want that kind of stuff, you better get a job, kid." That's what I did.

A good friend of mine worked for a paving company so I went and talked to the guy in charge about getting a job. I always looked older. Long hair. Ponytail. Goatee. "I'll tell you what," he said, "I'll give you 40 bucks a day. You ride here with Jim. You don't talk to any of my customers. If I catch you talking to a customer, I'm gonna tell them I don't know you and you're walking down the road man." I told him, "Hey, don't worry about it. Not a problem." So on the verge of 15 I was making 40 bucks a day, illegally. I shouldn't have been working on a pavement crew that's for sure. But I worked hard and I wore $100 sneakers and $150 jackets. I mean, what other 14-year-old kid was making a couple $100 a week? Then again, what other 14-year-old kid works 16-hour days?

One time we did this job down in Bristol and the paver broke. I had to push every wheelbarrow full of hot top down a quarter of a mile driveway. We usually started at 5:30 in the morning. We didn't even leave Bristol that night till 9:45. We finished up the job under the headlights of the truck. That was a long day.

There were quite a few of those long days. That's how I

work, long and hard. That's been my survival in life. I got that work ethic from my dad, because he was a hard-working man. People see you working really hard and people like that.

The crew definitely picked on me because I was younger, but they respected me. I was just a part of the group. They put me in the same category as a man and I enjoyed it. I got to be part of the adult conversations. Somebody would fire up a joint, "Here you go kid." I actually felt like I belonged.

I had been trying to quit school for a few years at that point. My probation officer kept making me go back. He said, "Once you're 16 there's nothing I can do about it." That's the legal age of emancipation. As soon as I turned 16, I quit school and started paving full-time, legally.

Working made me feel good. That's probably when I felt the most authentically me, whether it was in the woods with Dad or at the farm or paving. I just knew hard work was a part of me. I'd come home and I'd sleep sound at night. The days went pretty well when I was working.

I wasn't getting in as much trouble on the days I worked. I was still running the streets with my friends and ending up in jail for 72 hours on my off days. But during the week I wouldn't even go out. I was too tired. I'd drink at home instead. Once I started working, it was like I had a responsibility.

Working and making money made me feel good. I think I got a little too big for my britches. It made me feel a lot older and grown up than I really was. I thought I was an adult at 16. I had grown up fast and hard. I worked full time. I looked older, so stores never carded me. I could buy beer. I could buy cigarettes. I thought I had it made.

Fatherhood

I first met Melanie while I was dating her younger sister. Right off the bat, she was on me, like, "Oh, my god. He's so cute." She was easy to talk to and didn't expect a lot. When we started going together I was almost 17 and she was 20. She was all about her two kids – at the time; she made sure they came first. We clicked right off the bat.

Shortly after we got together, we weren't clicking any more. It was an abusive relationship. Quite a few times we had fistfights. I didn't mind that back then. That's the way I grew up. She'd whack a vacuum cleaner across my head or something; after that, I had no control. I don't know how we even stayed together.

I didn't know we were going to have a baby until four months before it happened. I had been using condoms until Melanie told me, "I hate them fuckin' things. I'm on birth control anyway," she said. "Don't worry about it."

I said, "You sure?"

"Yeah." and she showed me the little container of pills.

One day her friend slipped up and said something to me about Melanie being pregnant. I was in the bathroom shortly after and I found that little stupid pill container and not a one had been taken.

I felt blindsided. I thought, *my life is over. I might as well just die. At 17, I got a kid. I told myself, I can't be a parent. What do I have to offer a kid? Nothing. I can't even take care of myself. I can't pull my head out of the bottle long enough to give a shit whether I eat today or tomorrow or the next day, let alone take care of a kid. And I'm not much for changing diapers and all that shit.* It was just way too much. Everything went downhill from there.

Melanie and I would fight like cats and dogs. I don't know why we kept putting ourselves through that. I don't think we knew. I used to say, "I'll never be like my family. I'll never do that to my lady." But there I was, the kind of person I said I'd never be in life. It was crazy! For what? What did that prove? What did it get me? Nothing but shattered relationships.

A year after my daughter Sharon was born I asked my mother, "I don't know what to give a kid, especially a little girl. I don't have a goddamn clue. What do I do, Mom? I don't know how to give her what she needs. What the fuck! I don't even know how to get what I need!"

"I tell you what," my mother says to me, "Bring her up here and drop her off, Alton." My mother raised my daughter from then on.

While Sharon was growing up at my parents' house we were more like brother and sister than father and daughter. I'd come over to visit maybe once a week and crash after a party. Mostly, I was here, there, and everywhere. She was always happy when I'd come home for a day. I do remember she liked to draw and do coloring books. I really didn't see a lot of her childhood. Looking back on it, it really shows me how much I missed in her life. All of it. I missed her whole life. No wonder she hates me. Today she doesn't want anything to do with me. I really don't blame her.

The next time Melanie got pregnant, I had actually kind of grown up some. We had an apartment. I had a job. Things seemed all right. We had a son, Alton, Junior. Then a year later I found out Melanie hadn't been paying the rent, so we were kicked out of our apartment. Shortly after that we broke up. It was a nasty time.

Alton stayed with his mother. I wish I'd taken him with me. He saw a lot of stuff kids that age shouldn't see. At just three years old he'd get up on the counters and run around saying, "Fuck you. Fuck you, you fucker, you fuckin' fuck," and stuff like that. The people she hung out with would egg him on, thinking that was cool to hear him say stupid shit like that. I couldn't stand it. I stopped bothering to visit him. I didn't want to see it anymore. I wanted to hit him.

I pushed myself away from my kids. I saw too much of myself in my son. It wasn't his fault. I'd do anything to take that back if I could. I'd put more of my focus towards making sure my kids had a decent life, instead of always thinking, "Am I gonna get high today? What am I drinking today?"

I didn't think I was worthy of being a father. I wasn't worth anybody loving me like a kid would love a father. I'd never done anything to deserve that kind of love. I think it put a big distance between my kids and me. Why I would ever hold that kind of resentment against my kids, I don't know. But I did.

I Hit a Deer

Any day I wasn't working, I was at the bar by ten o'clock in the morning and clean the tables and sweep the floors. I'd throw people out or I'd bartend, whatever they needed. In exchange, the woman who owned the bar would give me a tab. I could get draft beers for 50 cents a piece and drink till three, four o'clock in the afternoon. I'd drink 50 beers throughout the day like it was water. For quite a while I just stopped working.

For a year and a half I went to the bar every day, from ten in the morning till closing time. Besides having a tab, there were 25 or 30 different people that frequented the bar and anytime they came in, "Hey, Alton wants a drink." I could go to the bar with ten cents in my pocket and get hammered all day. Most of the time I didn't even have to work. People would ask me, "Hey you want to do this?" Anytime I got my hands on drugs I'd sell enough to cover what I wanted. Then I'd do the rest. That was my daily life. Drinking, drugs, and fighting.

One night the bar owner needed me to help the music guy run the karaoke. "You can't drink a lot while you're doing it," she told me, "but next time you come in I'll run you a tab." I'm like, score!

He was there that night, the one that used to rape me. When I saw him, I walked right over to his table. That was my first reaction. I was going to pick the table up and kill him with it. Then I thought, *if I do that I have to explain myself. Why would I attack somebody out of the blue like that, somebody that nobody's ever had a problem with? I thought, I'll kill him some other day when nobody's around. But seeing him set me on edge.*

I was helping run the karaoke and this woman started getting pissed off about a song. I don't even know what her problem was. I told her, "Go shut your mouth and sit down cause nobody really cares. I, for one, don't. Fucking beat it." She went back to her table and got her boyfriend and his friends all worked up too.

Her boyfriend came up and tried to tackle me around the waist. Two of his friends grabbed my arms, one on each side. I was trying to fight myself away from them. This friend of mine, Francis, came over and started punching me in the face while I was being held. I was friends with these guys and they're holding me down and punching me. I looked down and under the karaoke set up was a two-by-four. I got my arm away from one of the guys holding me. I grabbed that two-by-four and I smashed the other guy right upside the head. Smash! And he let go. I wasn't held down anymore and Francis knew he was getting one, so he started running away.

That's where I should have stopped. I wasn't really hurt that bad. It was more about my pride and ego. From there, my mind just went black.

My sister Laurie came up to me. She could see I was headed out the door after these two guys. She tried to talk to me, and I didn't even know her. I wrapped my hand right up in her hair and grabbed her by the ass of her pants and I wound her, just like a piece of four-foot wood, right over a table. "Get the fuck away from me. I don't even know who you are." My rage was so heavy; I couldn't recognize my own sister.

I ran outside after these two guys just to beat the hell out of them. That was my intention. But Francis wouldn't come back and fight me because nobody was there to hold me back. I even threw the two-by-four to him. I said, "Here, you're gonna need this dude. You might want to use it." He just hovered there, ready to run. I said, "No, pick it up. Let's go. Both of you retards. You think you're gonna hold me, and punch me and all that shit? Now it's on. What are you gonna do?" They wouldn't fight me. "If you don't come back here… Dude, I know where you live. You want me to show up there for you?" They took off in the girl's car.

Something snapped. I went inside and grabbed Stacy, the girl that I was with, and I dragged her right out of the bar. I threw her in the passenger seat of her own car and proceeded to drive down the road. I was headed to Francis' house. Up ahead, his girlfriend had stopped her car on the centerline of the road, with no lights on. Francis stepped out in the road. I don't know what he thought he was going to do. Fight me while I'm driving down the road? I was driving and I was pissed. The accelerator was floored. All of a sudden, I saw this car in the middle of the road. I swerved and hit Francis at 55 miles an hour. His head came in through the windshield. I hit him so hard he almost touched the telephone wires. It ripped his boots off his feet. They found one of his cowboy boots 50 feet in the woods, and those things don't come off easy. He was in the ditch unconscious when they picked him up in an ambulance. They took him to the hospital and stapled his head up and put him in a half-body cast.

I can't tell you to this day if I swerved to avoid hitting the car or if I swerved to hit him. I don't know. It's like there's a light switch. Once that light switch gets shut off I don't know people. I don't even know my own family. All I know is I'm killing something. And I'll beat myself to get to you.

After I hit Francis I went home. I was flipping. I was really freaking out. I called my father. I told him how glad I was that I killed this fucker. That must have been something crazy for him to hear. "Hey Dad, I just killed somebody and it was the best thing I've ever done."

Next thing I know there's eight cruisers blowing up on the lawn with dogs and guns. I ran out the back door and jumped out over the fence as far as I could. I ducked down underneath the alder trees and stayed there, hoping they wouldn't find me in the darkness.

They went by me five times with the dogs, didn't even smell me. I heard them on the radio saying, "Yeah, there's nothing here. We need to look somewhere else." Then I heard, "Well, we're gonna do one more walk around." I heard the radio getting closer so I knew that they were coming around.

One of the cops tripped on something in the lawn. He fell down on one knee. His hand landed right on my sneaker. Next thing I know, I have a dog in one ear and gun in the other. I said, "Get your dog away from me or I'll kill it. I'll force you to shoot me." The dog was still barking in my ear. "Get your fucking dog out of my ear or I'll rip its fucking throat out. I'm telling you. I'll force you to shoot me. Have you ever shot somebody? I bet you haven't. Do you want to? Cause you're gonna." Finally they got the dog away from me and I got up and was arrested.

They put me in the car and took me down to the station.

A cop came in and said, "This guy might not make it through the night."

I'd had about four hours to calm down by this point. I said, "What guy?"

"What do you mean, 'what guy?'"

I told him, "I hit a deer."

"You hit a deer?"

"Yeah. I hit a deer."

"A six-foot-two man? How do you get a deer out of that?"

"Well, it's like this. The last I saw was . . . " and I put my hands up by my head, like I might if something was coming at me, a lot like a set of antlers. "Looks like a deer to me. Don't it to you?"

"Put me back in my cell. I got nothing for you. What do you want me to do? Give the guy a hug? Sing a song? Hold his hand? What do you want from me?"

Then I sat in jail for seven months waiting to go to trial.

Trouble In-Between

I thought I did society a favor taking out that piece of shit. I thought I'm the knight in shining armor. I felt great. I said I should have backed up over his head. I know that doesn't sound logical, but that was how I was then.

While I was sitting in jail I found out Francis had threatened my family. So I sent him a message. "Let me tell you what. This isn't over. They're not keeping me in here forever dude. So you gonna move out of Maine? What you gonna do? If my family even comes out of your mouth again, you're done." I said, "I will take you and I will finish you." I wish I'd never said that. I had already done enough to the guy, way more than any person deserves. But I was really hostile about the whole situation.

After I had sobered up my sister came to see me at the jail. She told me, "If you ever put your hands on me like that, I'll kill you. While you're sleeping, I'll cut your throat out. Don't you ever, ever put your hands on me like that."

I said, "What are you talkin' about?"

She told me how I had picked her right up and threw her over a table during the fight at the karaoke bar. I didn't even have a clue. I didn't remember doing that. It was a blind rage, almost psychopathic really. I had no limits. I also didn't remember the conversation on the phone with my father that night. I didn't even remember what happened in the car either. The only reason I know what happened that night is because

Stacy told me. That poor girl had nightmares for five months. She wasn't the same after that.

I sat in jail for seven months waiting to go to prison. One day I looked out my cell door and there's my ex-girlfriend Melanie sitting in the visiting room in an orange jumpsuit in handcuffs. I sat there wondering, "What the hell? If she's in here, who's with the kids? What's going on?" So I got on the phone and called my mother. I asked if she could go check on the kids.

Turns out Melanie had taken off in her friend's truck. She was drunk and high, and left the kids in the apartment with this guy. As she was leaving she drove right into the side of the apartment, almost right into somebody's living room. She backed up and took off. In the meantime, a friend of mine lived next door. He heard the kids screaming like a herd of elephants. He had to get up early for work so he went over to tell them to shut up. The door was open a crack. He went in and saw Melanie's friend chasing the kids around with no pants on. So he got the kids out of the apartment and called the cops. The cops were there asking questions when Melanie came back with this guy's truck all smashed up. She was so drunk she could barely walk. She thought she had to fight them. So, there's my son Alton watching the cops beat his mother up.

I asked my sister, "Can you get Alton out of there – I'm waiting to go to prison. I'm going away for a couple years. When I get out, I'll straighten my act up and I'll get custody. And I'll take him from you."

She told me, "Alright, Alton, I'll do that. I don't want to see the kid go through this." So she took in Alton for two years.

My lawyer cost me a lot of money, a $4,000 retainer. My nieces and nephews even went blueberry raking to pitch in for it. I'm thankful they did, because he's a good lawyer. I just went in and pled guilty. At first they wanted to give me ten years. My lawyer talked to the DA and they came back with this offer of 18 months. I took it. They scheduled my sentencing hearing and they actually let me have post conviction bail till then. My boss came and bailed me out, $55,000 cash. I was out for three weeks.

While I was out on bail waiting to go to prison, I was driving, like an idiot. I knew I shouldn't have been; they took away my right to have a license long ago. It was the middle of winter, slippery. A cop pulled me over. He said I didn't maintain control of my vehicle. I said, "Whatever."

I figured the 18-month deal was off. I thought I was going away for a long time. They only added another six months to my sentence for that driving charge. Somehow, I really got lucky in this whole thing. On March 19, 2002 I was officially convicted and went to prison.

Here For a Good Time

Prison smelled like feet and armpits. Sometimes they had to force people to take a shower. At night it sounded like a zoo. People hooting and hollering all night. I'd hear them hollering at the guards, "Fuck you copper." Stupid shit. Often I'd lay in my bunk thinking about what I was going to do when I got out. I told myself, *I'm gonna get out and be clean. I'm done with this shit.*

I served most of my time at the Bolduc Correctional Facility, a minimum-security facility in Warren. It wasn't a bad place. It was better than the Maine Youth Center anyway. They had a full gym, a weight room, and a softball field. I read and slept a lot. I didn't have a very hard time in prison. If you kept to yourself and respected other people – you got to keep your neck. I didn't think it was that bad. But then again, I was used to being locked up as a kid.

My first job at Bolduc was making lunches for the guys on work release. We'd throw a couple pieces of slimy bologna in between two slices of bread with a mustard packet, little bag of chips and an orange or an apple. It was really bad the days we had egg salad and tuna fish.

Eventually I got into a work release program and worked building wire lobster traps. I didn't like it at first. My boss caught me in the corner with one of the girls that worked there. We were just hugging. She was married. He was pissed. You could see it in his face. When it was time for my review he had a big attitude with me. He said, "Yeah, man, you're not putting out enough pieces. I'm not giving you a raise." It took him a while to let stuff go. Eventually he gave me a raise and let me work overtime. I sent most of the money I earned home to my girlfriend at the time to help take care of her and her kids.

We weren't supervised too closely. Technically we weren't supposed to smoke cigarettes. Some guys would arrange to have friends drop stuff off at the work site by the side of the road at night. It would look just like a bag of trash. As soon as we got there in the morning, one of us would run up by the road and grab the bag. It'd be full of tobacco or cigarettes. Then before the big boss came in we'd sneak out back for a cigarette. The boss really didn't seem to care, as long as we smoked where nobody could see us, and we were back inside when the bell rang. But if one of us looked like we were trying to leave they called the mob squad right in.

There were lots of guys in prison just like me. We laughed and joked. That part of it was actually fun. Most of my friends were older guys. I didn't really hang out with the younger people. Those are the guys that really think they've got something to prove. I wasn't into that. I told them "I'm not here for a long time. I'm here for a good time." That was my saying.

The guys I made friends with had been in there for a long time, guys like Bob Ingerson and old Ray Rolls. They didn't make friends with very many people. They didn't even want to look at someone that would be getting out in two years. That's just the way it is. Bob Ingerson and his wife married really young. One night they were drunk and got in a fight and he stabbed her to death. He'd been in prison since 1962.

Bob and I would play dominos for hours. One day Ray and Bob and I were taking a break from dominos and Bob got his photo album from his cell. He showed me photos of his son. He supported his son from prison. His son had accepted him even after what he did. Bob was up for a parole hearing. He had a place to live. He owned a piece of land. He had a vehicle. He had a fully-grown son that wanted his father back, no matter what he'd done. He wanted to get to know his father. They denied Bob again. But that was the system. Bob died trying to get out on parole.

The day I got out of prison was great. I had my stuff all packed the night before. I had breakfast at Moody's Diner in Waldoboro first thing after I got out. I had a fucking great big six-egg omelet with bacon and green peppers and onions. They make good omelets there!

I had a good feeling about getting out. It was a familiar feeling for me. I'd be locked up for a while in jail or prison and when I got out, I'd always have that same feeling. My guts would be spinning. It was the thrill of freedom mingled with nervous possibilities. I thought I had all my affairs in order. My main plan was just to stay away from the drugs. I didn't think of anything else.

I wasn't even out for six months before I started driving shit up my nose again. It didn't take me very long to fall.

Telling the Secret

I was really pissed off at the world. They made me take four years of anger management and substance abuse counseling as part of my probation. The counselor I was going to was the first person in the world I ever told about being molested. It took her a long time to get it out of me. I was just blowing smoke up her ass every time I went in there – $90 a session. One day she looked at me, and she said, "There's something else in there."

I said, "There's nothing in there."

"There is and we're going to get to the bottom of it. You're mandated to be here by your probation officer. You're going to keep paying me $90 a week for me to sit here and look at you until you're ready."

For three weeks I just went in and sat there staring at her. Finally I blew up. I told her, "You want to know something? Man, sit your ass down and listen. Grab yourself some fucking tissues. You're going to need it. Let's do this." I was spitting out at her, veins sticking out of my head. A couple of times I thought I might pick her up and throw her out her own window. But she sat right there. I blew up for half an hour. It was bad. I couldn't control it anymore. My whole body was shaking. Finally when I got it all out. She said, "See, how does that feel?"

In some weird way, I actually felt better. At the same time, this woman now knew the darkest secret I've ever had in my life. Because of that, I thought she held a lot of power over me. I wasn't comfortable with that at all. Still, for some strange reason, I actually felt better.

She asked me, "Have you talked to your mother?"

"What are you stupid? I haven't told anybody in my life. Just you."

"Well, I think you should."

"Naw. I'm good on that."

A number of years later I worked up the courage and said to hell with it. I said to my mom, "Sit down and let me make you a coffee." We had a coffee, and I said, "You ever wonder why I was such a fucked up, twisted kid?"

She says, "I wondered that for a long time."

Then I told her. I told her everything, and I watched about ten years coming off my mother's life. She really took it to heart. She didn't show it on the outside, but I could see it. It made me wish I'd never told her. It made me wish I'd never said anything. I just watched the years leave her. She was mortified. I think she started to blame herself for it. After all, she dropped me off there every day. She didn't know she was putting me in that situation. She was just trying to go to work, help provide for us.

She took it like it was all her fault, which was not what I was trying to do. I was just trying to do what my counselor said I should do, which to me, wasn't that great of an idea. I felt like I did something wrong by telling her. I really kind of beat myself down. Putting something like that on her shoulders to worry about was not very fair of me I don't think. She had enough to worry about besides a 25-year-old kid boo-hooing.

I do think she had a new understanding of me and what I'd been through, but I think that hurt her worse than wondering. I could see it was really eating at her. I know she wanted to talk about it, but back then, talking to me was like talking to a wall. You'd actually be better off trying to talk to a wall. At least the wall's not going to throw a chair across the room. I wish I hadn't told her.

It's all hindsight. Looking back, maybe it was the right thing to tell her, no matter how it made her feel. She had a right to know that. Still it didn't make it any more comfortable.

Louise

I started dating Louise while I was out on bail, before I went to prison. She saw my sister at the bar after the whole big mess and said, "Oh, when you see Alton, give him my phone number. Tell him to give me a call. I feel bad for what happened." So I called her. It just went on from there. At that time the relationship felt like something beautiful in the ugliness of my life, something stable. I'd never really had that kind of support. I thought *this is something I could really grab onto*. But it turns out that wasn't a good enough reason to get married. I found that out the hard way.

When I look back on my life and see all of the mistakes I made, it kind of makes me laugh to see how stupid some of these mistakes really were.

Louise and I got married shortly after I got out of prison. We had our own little apartment and my son Alton came to live with us. That was the happiest I ever saw Alton. Things went really well for the first few months. She had a son that was around the same age as Alton. They got along great. They'd come to me and want to play cars. We'd take the boys to Sears Island, go swimming in the ocean, light a fire right on the beach and cook marshmallows with the boys. It was a pretty good time. Those first few months of marriage were pretty cool.

There was a big difference in our ages. I was 25 and Louise was 41 when we got married. After awhile she started acting like a mother to me, telling me what to do. She got angry with me because I wouldn't slap her older son, who was 15 years old. She wanted me to discipline him. I told her, "What? Are you fucking insane? I'm not gonna put my hands on your kid. I'm not doing that shit. You're crazy. I'll talk to him, but I'm not doing that."

She even called California and put this kid's father on the phone to say, "I don't understand if you're a man why wouldn't you discipline the child?" I'm thinking, *Are all you people stupid? Why would I take another man's kid and hit him? I'm not into that. I don't even hit my own kid.* That started our wars.

During my time in prison I told myself the drugs just weren't worth it anymore. That whole scene just isn't cool. I got out and things were going really well for a while. I took a pile of classes while I was in prison. I thought I had the world by the balls. I could stay away from that stuff. But I didn't.

I started doing carpentry work with a couple of people that did drugs. Before I knew it, I was stopping on the way to work to pick up an 8 ball of cocaine. I'd sit at work and smoke crack all day. Some days we wouldn't even work; we'd sit in the car and get high. That's all it took to take me out of my positive mode and get right back into the same bullshit mode I'd been all my life. But for just a hint of time I actually felt positive.

Louise was really gullible; it's the only thing that really kept our marriage going as long as it did. One time, I'd been smoking crack all day. The crew didn't even go to work that day. We sat in the driveway of the job site and smoked a quarter ounce of cocaine. I went home and was really just geeked right out of it. I couldn't sit down. My eyes were all funky. I couldn't stop pacing. Louise asked me, "What are you on? Are you on crystal?" That's what they do in California, I guess.

I told her, "No."

"What the hell is wrong with you?"

"Oh, Ron, the guy I work with, he gave me some Benadryl or some cold medicine or something." I said, "Yeah. I can't take those anymore cause it really messes me up."

"Yeah, you shouldn't do that. You don't look good."

"Yeah."

It was just little things like that. I didn't have to worry about going home because I could make up something. I'm pretty quick on my feet.

After I started back on the cocaine I just didn't have it in me any more to keep up the relationship. We started growing apart. We were fighting a lot. I let my marriage fall apart. One day I went upstairs and I told her, "You know, I'm fucking leaving. I'm done with your mouth. I can't do it. I don't need another mother. Eat shit. I'm outta here." I started down the stairs and she broke the cordless phone over my head. I went downstairs and grabbed Alton. "Dude, let's blister out of here. I'm done with it."

We went outside and just walked around the apartment building. I talked with Alton. I calmed down a lot. We went back in and things were a little better for a while.

About three weeks later Louise and I got into another big argument. This time I actually did leave. I told her, "See you later. I'm done. Our marriage: nah. We're gonna get this shit annulled and you're out of my face." I grabbed Alton. I took off out the door. She took off running down the block. Well, she went to the neighbors and called the cops. She told them I pushed her down the stairs, slapped her and broke all the phones so she couldn't make a phone call. The cops came and arrested me for it.

Her own son was like, "Are you guys dumb? The only person that's ever hit anybody here is my mother. My mother hits him."

The cop that came and arrested me put his head down and said, "Alton, I can't even believe I'm here doing this."

"Well, I can't either." I said, "I haven't even done anything."

"I know. I was in the house. There wasn't any sign of a struggle. All the phones seemed like they were all intact. They worked. I picked them up. The phones are all working. There are no bruises. There's no bleeding. There's nothing showing anybody got pushed down a set of stairs."

They still arrested me for it. But the DA and the cops, they all saw right through it. The case was thrown out of court but our marriage was over.

I never looked back, not even for a second. She called me one night and asked me, "How the hell can you do this to me?

How can you do this to me?"

I told her, "Man, you did it to yourself." I hung up the phone, right then I just knew that I didn't care. I didn't care what other people thought or their feelings, none of it.

Every day was just shit. But by evening it was worse. That seemed like the story of my life. How can you get worse than shit? I decided for the third time in my life I was just gonna drink myself to death. Cause who gives a shit anyway? I don't. And I'm gonna use all the drugs I can get my hands on. And some day it'll be all over.

Ellis Pond

I went camping at this little pond, a beautiful place called Ellis Pond. I like to go kayaking there sometimes. I grabbed some alcohol and a little bit of get high. Louise's case against me had been thrown out of court. I had just been released from jail and Louise and I were done. I was there to be by myself.

Joe, a friend of mine, and his wife, Shelly, showed up to go swimming while I was there. I met Joe years before when it was raining on his wedding day. I must have spent $400 on tarps to make a dry place for their wedding. We got to be friends after that. We'd go fishing together sometimes.

The day they showed up at Ellis Pond, Joe asked me, "You mind if we back in and hang out with you for a little while and go swimming? Turn the radio on in the truck?"

I said, "I don't give a shit what you do Joe. Go right ahead."

I had a little fire going. I had a little cordless skill saw that I was cutting the wood with. We're sitting there, and Shelly starts talking to me about my sister owing her money. I tried to pay her. I said, "Look here. Just shut the fuck up. Cause I don't want to hear it. I'm not out here for this shit. I'm really not." I said, "I'm out here trying to be by myself and have a good evening. I want to get drunk and I want to beat my head off the trees. Just leave me alone. Here's your money. Shove it in your ass. I don't care what you do with it. So, fucking shut your mouth cause I'm done hearing it." That's when she slapped me.

A little while later she starts getting weird on me, hitting on me, and her husband's right there. I told her, "Don't fucking touch me again." Before I knew it she slapped me again. I told Joe, "Look, if your wife even staggers and bumps into me one more time tonight, I'm fucking smashing you both. And I'm telling you, you better hang on and you better be ready." Then Shelly punched me in the side of the face. I came after him and Joe picked up his shovel. He actually hit me with a shovel, like 35 times, like a baseball bat, and I'm still coming at him.

I picked up my skill saw and I said, "You want to play?" I lifted up the guard and I went towards his face. I was going to cut him up. I was gonna kill him is what I was gonna do. I was so mad; I could have killed him right there and not even felt bad about it. I told him, "I tried to warn you guys. I tried and I tried, and I tried some more and it didn't work. So now I'm gonna turn you into fish food."

It was just a bad night. It was a bad night turned even worse. That seemed like the story of my life.

They pressed charges and we went to trial. They couldn't prove their case. I actually won the trial. Joe and I are friends again now. It was just a really weird time in my life. People didn't matter to me then. You could be my best friend, but when the time comes, I snap and I don't know you anymore. You take things to the extreme and that's what happens. That's how my temper was, animalistic, kind of psychotic I guess. Today, looking back, I can see I was never an animal at all; I was only human and didn't know it.

Someone to See Through My Lies

I actually met my girlfriend Ronda in jail. She got arrested for a driving charge, operating after revocation. I was there waiting to go to trial on the Ellis Pond assault. Back then the men and women actually had recreation time together, plus there were other activities like AA meetings and church groups that were co-ed. Now it's a lot different. They don't let you do that anymore.

We first started talking a little bit during AA meetings. Then it went to passing notes. I could climb the walls in our shower room, look through the vent, and actually see into their dayroom. We'd roll notes up and pass them through the vent. That's how it started.

We talked about everything, from drugs to violence, to everything. The first note, I mentioned drugs and she wrote back, "I don't dig on that shit really." So I didn't think it was going to work out very good between us. But two days after she got out, I got a letter from her. Next day I got another letter, and the next day I got another letter. She'd write about how things were going in her life on Indian Island. What she was doing. Asking, "How are things going for you? " We started writing about life and kids and goals--stuff I never really talked to people about before.

We wrote back and forth. Then when I got out we really hit

it off. I kept the drugs away from her. I knew she wouldn't like it one bit, which in the end was good for me.

I told Ronda when we first got together, "I'm really fuckin' screwed up." I told her things to watch out for about me. If such and such happens or if you see me acting a certain way, "there's a good chance I'm into the drugs." I gave her the information she needed to see through my lies. In the end, that saved me. Saved us.

Supplying the Habit

Again, I took a job doing carpentry when I got out of prison. After two and half years I decided to go into business for myself. I bought a house trailer in Swanville and renovated it. I thought I had the world by the short and curlies, but I was still spending three quarters of my money for drugs. I had to try to explain to Ronda where all of this money was going. Half the time I'd come home and say, "That's what I made," even if it was only $75 for the week. I actually made decent money for a while. The first year I made $35,000. It would have been good if I had put it to something that was worth putting money into.

I really thought *this is life. This is cool.* I could call myself self-employed. In the meantime, I had no health insurance. I had nothing; just what little bit of money I had left in my pocket after I did payroll and got high that day. I was working hard for nothing. It made me question my integrity. *Why are you even doing this? What's the sense? Are you trying to move forward? You just want to supply your habit?* I couldn't admit any of these ugly truths to myself then. I regressed inside myself. I only thought about me. That's all I really cared about.

I started cutting corners; I just didn't care. I didn't care how good the job came out or any of that. I cared about getting my money so I could get high. I took advantage of quite a few people. That's not something I can look back on and feel good about, that's for sure. It really makes me sad to think of the people I've taken advantage of. They trusted me. I guess I'm glad I'm not in that situation anymore.

Any work I get today I do it as good as I can. I do it because I want to survive. I want to have a place to live. I want to be able to have a car. I want to eat food. I want to have lights and heat and all that stuff. These may just be the basics, but it's more than that. It's self-respect for the life I can create.

Worst Day of My Life

My father got so sick he couldn't walk the length of the trailer without stopping to try to get a breath. The doctors told him he either had pneumonia or bronchitis. They gave him medicine for both. Finally, after two and a half years of it, Dad told them "You can shove your medicine in your ass, cause I'm done with it." So they sent him to a specialist.

January 19, 2009 was the worse day of my life. My parents stopped by my house and asked if we needed anything from the store. "Well, sure. I could take a ride to the store." I hadn't realized Dad had an appointment earlier with the doctor. On the way to the store they told me Dad had asbestos cancer. The doctor told him he'd be lucky to make it another six months.

On the way back from the store, we were talking just like normal, and all of a sudden my mother starts making weird noises. So Dad pulled into the trailer park where my friend lived. I almost jumped out of the moving van. I grabbed her up out of the front seat and carried her into my friend's place. I laid her on the floor and told my friend, "Call the ambulance. Get them here. Ask them how to do CPR cause I've never done it."

While we waited for the ambulance, 911 gave me instructions over the phone for CPR. I was able to keep her alive with a faint pulse. After about 25 minutes I couldn't feel a pulse anymore. There was no warm breath coming out of her body. I knew it was over.

My father kept begging me, "Just try one more time." So I did. I was holding on to my sanity by a thread at this point. He wanted me to try it one more time. "One more time, please." There were quite a few one more times.

I couldn't do it anymore. My body was giving up on me. My emotions were starting to take over. We could have had 15 people there doing CPR; she'd been down so long that even if we brought her back she would have been a vegetable. The ambulance finally arrived after 45 minutes. They pronounced her dead at the hospital.

At the hospital, we were waiting to go in and see her one last time and I made some promises to my dad. He said, "I know how you are. I know what this is gonna do to you. Don't let it. Don't let it." He knew I was heavy on the alcohol. He knew that if anything even remotely upset me I would turn to alcohol. I promised him I'd keep my head on my shoulders, and I did, as far as the alcohol went. I just slipped a little further into the drugs. He didn't know much about my drug problem. But I never promised anything about drugs. It would have been stupid to make that kind of promise. I knew that even on my best days there was no way I could have kept that kind of promise.

I was in shock for a long time after Mom died. I had nightmares for months. I would wake up crying. It was crazy. I'd never given anybody CPR in my life. I've never had anything like that happen to me before – my mother dying in my lap. I felt like a failure because I couldn't produce the CPR she needed. She had nitroglycerin right in her purse. I didn't even know she had it. I could have grabbed the nitroglycerin and stuck it under her tongue and drove to the hospital like my father wanted. She might still be alive.

In my mind, I started playing out all the reasons her death was my fault. My mother had suffered congestive heart failure a couple of times when I was a teenager. I blamed myself for that. When I was a kid and running the streets, she would sit by the phone and just wait and wait, carrying all this stress. If I had been a better kid . . . If I hadn't told her about getting molested . . .

I know it's not my fault. I didn't kill my mother. It took me quite a while to be able to tell myself that. I thought maybe I deserved to see her die for all the shit I put her through.

My sister once told me, "At least you got to see her before she died." I was pretty mad at her for saying that. I didn't want to watch her die. I didn't want to see her like that. Deep down I think my sister was probably right. At least I did get to see her at the end. I got to ride to the store with her. We saw one of my sisters at the store that day. She talked to mom. Everybody was laughing. Things were good. Then 20 minutes later the world fell apart. It shows you how quickly things can happen. How little control or power we have over these things.

I didn't give myself a chance to mourn. I told myself I had to be strong for everybody else, that I really didn't feel pain. You're not gonna feel nothing. But I felt it. I didn't like it. I didn't like that feeling. I didn't know how to even take that feeling, never mind admit it.

Parting Words

I used to think my father was part goat. I figured he would live forever. Dad's cancer was so progressed the chemo wasn't going to do anything. His pleura, the membranes around the lungs, were so thick they couldn't even put a needle through it to get a biopsy. It's supposed to be around the thickness of a bed sheet. They had to cut him open and take a piece out. The doctor said Dad had the heart and lungs of a 30 year old, but he must have been dealing with these symptoms for the last 30 years by the looks of the progression. He told my father, "Chemo might get you three or four more months, but how happy are those months gonna be?"

"Well, my wife's gone now anyway. Who gives a shit? I don't want no more months." He decided he was just going to wait it out.

It's kind of ironic. I remember my father telling people stories about things he'd done with asbestos, saying how surprised he was that he never contracted asbestosis. Asbestos is the best insulator known to man, but it's also the most deadly. Dad did mechanical insulation for many years. Usually he was hired to remove the asbestos and put in fiberglass. They'd beat it off the pipes. It was like paper-mache. The air would be right full of dust. One guy would be on the ground sweeping, and there'd be a couple people up top beating the shit off. After all those years of working with it he never had any symptoms, but he had it all the same.

I came by to see Dad at least once a day when he was

sick. We'd sit around the kitchen table and talk. In his last few months of his life we developed more of an actual relationship than I'd ever had with him. It was really weird. It took him till his deathbed to tell me he loved me. We developed the kind of bond we should have had all those years. It was hard for me. I still had a lot of anger inside me from so many years without ever a hint of his love. Then all of a sudden there's a pile of it.

During his last three months he slept in his hospital bed in the living room by the big bay window. My sister Laurie moved right into the house and took care of him. Anytime she couldn't do it, I'd come over and take care of him.

He started losing a lot a weight. He was around 245 pounds when my mother died and went down to 103 pounds by the end. He was just a wrinkled up old man. That was horrible. Every bit of dignity he had was stripped.

Finally, before he died he said he was proud of me. I had never heard that from him before. All my life I always tried to make Dad proud. It never worked out quite that way. I just never added up really. I was a wild kid.

I found out so much stuff about my father right before he died that it almost made me sick. I never knew any of this. Some of it I didn't like. This is how little connection or conversation we'd had between us. In the days leading up to his death, he didn't say a lot. But near the end he started hollering out names of people I had never even heard about before. "Allen! Allen!"

I thought he was calling out my name. "What Dad? What?

What's going on?" I could tell that he wasn't even with us anymore. I pulled my brother Dellas outside. Dellas is older. He was born in the 50s. He's known Dad for a long time. I asked him, "You know anybody named Allen?"

"Geeze, Dad must have never told you, eh?"

"What?"

Dellas told me Dad had three babies with his first wife that didn't survive. They were born with holes in their hearts. They survived for a little while, but they died young. He said, "Yeah, one of them, the boy, was Allen." I never knew any of this.

It was hard to watch my father die, to go from a happy energetic man to nothing. He could barely even move. He'd lift his arms and all the skin was hanging off. All you could see was a wrist bone and that's it.

We were all there with him when he passed – my sisters and my brothers. We took turns holding his hand. The night he died he wanted morphine. We knew he was dying. My sisters couldn't do it. So I gave him a shot of morphine and after that he got really calm and didn't say a lot. He just lay there almost comatose.

Dad died in October, just ten months after Mom. That was the saddest but happiest day of my life. It was sad that he was gone. But I was just so happy to not have to see him lying comatose in that hospital bed anymore. How you can feel that happy and sad at the same time? I didn't understand it.

Losing my parents made me think about my own life and death. I thought *I'd really like to be a little more like them, a little more caring.* It took me a long time to achieve even a piece of that. I was pretty clouded. In the middle of my drug riddled ramblings I would tell myself, *Jesus, being a little nicer would be good, or being able to express yourself to people, or even to have a connection with people would be great.* If I had had more of a connection with my parents I could have enjoyed all that time before they died. But I was too far within myself.

For the last half of his life my father was really a Christian man. There was a big change in him. He was all about helping people. He didn't do anything bad towards anybody. He'd give you anything. Maybe he tried to make up for some of the shit that he did earlier in his life.

If you were to ask any of my uncles or anybody that's ever known him to describe Beverly Lane. They'd say, "A man of very few words." And he was – especially with us. If he had to tell you more than once, it'd be ugly. We just avoided him. But later in his life he really dug right into church and took it to heart. He tried to live that, which I thought was pretty phenomenal.

Dad worked at Goodwill during his last years and really loved it. I don't even understand it. He just loved working with the people. He was one of the guys that accepted the donations and put the tags on the items. He became a social butterfly in his way. If you go in there today and talk to a couple of the people he worked with and mention Bev, I bet they'd be like, "Oh my God. I loved Bev so much." He really did change. At the end of his life, he changed a lot.

I've often wondered, "Is this the end of my life? Is that why I'm changing so much?" That's what happened to my father. At least if I die tomorrow, I'll know I made a change.

Family War Zone

I used to tell my son, "When you turn 18, Mr. Man, you and me. It's on! You're getting it. Don't think you're not. There's nothing gonna stop it." Those were my words to him. "When you're 18, you're gonna find out. You push me and push me and push me. I can't do nothing now. But guess what? When you're of age, I can do something." That was my logic. Not very logical. I can see that now.

I put my kids in foster care. I forced the authorities to put them in foster care. I couldn't handle them. I didn't have the capacity to deal with my problems, never mind their problems. At the same time, my mind was clouded by excessive drug use. Anytime I could I was getting high, trying to get away from my problems. I didn't want to deal with it. I made a lot of poor choices. If I wasn't as high as I could be, or if I wasn't drunk all the time, maybe things might have been different – maybe not.

Sometimes I think the drugs are the only thing that kept me sane, the only thing that kept me grounded enough to not lash out and be violent--because that's what I wanted to do so bad. I don't even know how I stopped myself from assaulting my kids.

My daughter, Sharon, was introduced to a whole new world after the death of her grandmother, the woman who had raised her. My father was dying of asbestos cancer. He said, "I can't do it. I can't take care of her. I'm almost bedridden. I can barely take care of myself." So Sharon came to live with Ronda, Alton Jr., my step-children, and me.

Ronda did her best to welcome my kids into the family. She used to take Sharon along with her own daughters to the mall for a girls' day. When Sharon found out we had rules and that she had to actually follow the rules, plain and simple, she started making problems.

All of a sudden, my kids started treating Ronda like shit. I don't understand why you would treat somebody like shit because they have rules in their house. Before long we were butting heads all the time. There was no peace at all in my house.

Sharon was going through a difficult time in life and had just lost the closest thing to a loving mother she had, her grandmother. I didn't know how to deal with my own emotions, never mind a teenage girl's feelings.

She started doing things and saying things that were seriously hurting other people in our family. I just wasn't interested in the bullshit anymore. My house was like a war zone, between me and Ronda, between me and the kids, between the kids and Ronda.

Every morning I lay in bed wishing I didn't have to wake up, thinking of what I'd have to listen to that day. The situation was volatile. I resented my kids. That's how I felt. Finally, I said I was done with Sharon. She eventually got into a foster home and seems to be doing well there, though we don't communicate directly.

I really didn't support Sharon through this time--not at

all. Not like a father should have. I pushed her away from me. "Who are you? I don't even know you anymore. What's your name? Who's your parents? I never met you."

It cost a lot. It really cost a lot, and I don't mean money-wise . . . it's hard to think about some times.

Things with my son Alton were also going down hill. Ronda liked to remind me that I was the one who taught him to bullshit. Even on the days that he had been grounded, I'd say to him, "Dude, I want to get out of this fucking house. Let's go. You keep your mouth shut." We'd go down to my neighbors. I'd drink like a fish and Alton would run wild, playing with the neighborhood kids. I wouldn't even pay attention half the time. Later on Ronda would come home. Alton would be in bed. I'd be hammered on the couch. But I taught him how to lie, how to say, "That never happened. I've been in my room all day. What do you mean? We never left the house."

"How did your father get drunk?"

"I don't know."

The line of bullshit seemed to hold until one day she found mud on the bottom of his pants while doing the laundry. He wasn't supposed to leave the house because he was grounded.

"Alton, how'd you get mud on the bottom of your pants?"

"I don't know."

Ronda liked to remind me sometimes: "The kid's lying, it's

your fault. You taught him how."

Teaching that kid to lie was the stupidest thing I've ever done in my life, and I've done a lot of stupid stuff. I've never been much of a father figure or a good role model. If anybody followed me they were crazy.

Alton's behavior at home and at school was getting pretty bad. He wouldn't listen. He'd steal. He'd talk back to you. The school was calling me every day of the week saying, "Come pick him up." He used to like to go four-wheeling. So, I told him, "I tell you what. You give me a month with none of this 'come pick me up' shit going on I'll buy you a four-wheeler. You're old enough now." So he made it through a month and I bought him a four-wheeler. The kid rode it three times. Even things that he really seemed to enjoy didn't matter. He just didn't care.

I really thought I hated him. I didn't want to ever see him again. Because, if I did I was gonna smack him. It was just too much. Fighting everyday. The cops were bringing him home all the time. He was breaking into my neighbors' places looking for cigarettes all the time, scaring old ladies.

I kept asking every one of his school counselors and case management people to do something. Every person that came to my house, supposedly to work with this kid, I asked them all, "Can you help me? I'm on my frayed ends of sanity right now. Can you help me get him into some residential treatment? Something?" Everybody told me oh, yeah, yeah, yeah. But nothing ever happened. Nothing.

Finally after two and half years of asking for help I said to his guidance counselor, "You and I need to talk. Your office. Let's go." I told her, "You know how I've been asking you guys for help for two and half years? I'm at my wit's end. Let me tell you this way. You're either gonna help me, or I'm gonna go home tonight and I'm spending about 20 minutes in the room with him, and I can't guarantee his safety. I really can't. I'm so fed up with it. I look at the kid and I want to hit him. You know? I've been asking you people. Now what are you gonna do to help me?"

She's like, "Well . . ."

I said, "No man, I'm serious. I'm dead serious. You want to think about this and you want to tell me what we're gonna do."

She said, "You know, we'll see if we can get him in Acadia."

"Good enough." I said, "Good. That's all I've been asking for."

Acadia is a psychiatric hospital in Bangor that works with kids. After only a week there, I get a phone call saying Alton's ready to be discharged on Tuesday. "Really? He hasn't even been in there a week! What have you really done to help this kid in under a week?"

"Well sir, he is ready to be released."

"No he's not."

"Sir, he will be released tomorrow morning."

"Well, you're gonna be releasing him to himself, because I'm not doing it. I asked you for help, now you're gonna drop him back in my lap. Can you help him or not?" I said, "As a matter of fact, you know what? I'm gonna force you to help him. I'm not picking him up. I'm not doing it. Help him. Get him some help. I can't do it. What the hell do you want from me?"

I didn't pick him up, so they put him in foster care. I made myself look like a bad person, but I really didn't care any more about all that. It would look even worse if I beat the hell out of my kid. I figured it was now or never. He's gonna be living outside if he keeps it up.

Our family didn't feel very much like a family. It felt like my own kids were against me. I didn't really understand what I had done to them to make them be against me like that. I really didn't think I did anything to deserve that. But apparently they did. That's the story of the relationship with my children.

Quiver on the Floor

I was 13 years old when my mother's doctor wrote her a prescription for Percocet. She wouldn't take them. So I did. In those pills I found a way to have goodness in my life, even if it was fleeting. There is no sorrow. There is no pain. There is no, "boohoo is me." None of that stuff. Later I got into other drugs. I had a big fetish with cocaine. I loved cocaine. I liked them all. Everything I tried I liked.

When I was about 18, right after I found out I was going to be a father; some friends brought some bags of heroin from Massachusetts to sell for $25 or $30. I had always told myself I'd never try heroin. One night I wanted an 8 ball of cocaine and I couldn't find any cocaine. A friend of mine came by. "I've got some of this H."

"Man I don't know about all that." Yet I was tempted. "Well, what the hell. Give me some." I tried it. It made me sick, but I fell right in love with it.

I used to go over to a friend's house to party. In the wintertime the snow bank off his deck looked like a rainbow. People drinking Kool-Aid and doing heroin, eventually they'd have to puke. So they'd go out of the house and throw-up over the steps. It was really gross. The snow bank looked like it had fruit loops all over the place, different colors, reds and oranges and purples.

After I got out of prison I switched from cocaine and heroin to opiate painkillers. I stopped snorting cocaine because it didn't have the same effect. I found that OxyCotton[2] gives you kind of the same buzz as heroin, but it was a lot easier to find. Everybody had it. Old ladies had prescriptions and didn't even take them. I'd talk to some of my friends' grandmothers about their meds. I told them I was in pain too. "I'll give you $20 a piece for those." They didn't think about addiction. They just think it's medicine for pain. It makes them sick so either they're going to throw it away, or maybe they could sell it to me. "Twenty dollars? Really?"

I'd take two oxy-80 pills, crunch them up in a pile and snort it right in one line. It would make me sick. I'd be puking all over the place afterwards. But it did the job. It made me forget all about this world.

I went to the doctor's one day. "Look, my finger aches. My elbows ache. My knees hurt. My hips. What the hell is going on?" He told me I had arthritis and wrote me a prescription for Percocet. I filled up on 200 of the 15-milligram pills, which was supposed to last me a month. I snorted 100 of them in three days. Then I was out chasing more. I don't really know what I thought I was trying to achieve by snorting all these painkillers?

I've done the quiver on the floor many times from needles with heroin mixed with cocaine. I'd get so wasted I was shaky. I was so shaky I couldn't hit myself again. I just couldn't find the vein. I'd end up pushing that stuff in my arm. Then it's right in the muscle and it would bruise. So I'd ask my friend, "Hey, Hit me." This guy did crazy shots. He put so much in there, you

2   OxyCotton is the street name for OxyContin used to treat severe pain.

couldn't even use cotton to suck it up. Boom. I was right on the floor as soon as he got it in me. I would be convulsing. He'd be on top of me. Slapping me in the face. Dumping water on me. As soon as I came back and kind of got my bearings, "Man! Give me another one! I gotta have another one of those, that was pretty good." What a feeling.

I didn't want to live, so I said, "Put a little more in there." I knew a lot of people who died of an overdose. It seemed like a pretty peaceful way to go. You get a real good high. Then there's no more. What better way to go--for a drug addict? I always chased that. I wanted to be dead before I was 25.

PART II

Eyes Open

I thought I kept my drug problem pretty well hidden. I really didn't want the kids to see me doing that. I'd go out to the shed or I'd tell Ronda, "Hey, I gotta go pick up some scrap metal." Then I'd jump in my dump truck, take off and snort pills somewhere. I wouldn't get home until evening. She thought I was legitimately out there trying to make money. Some of the time I was. Most days, I was snorting around 30 pills a day.

Ronda knew something was going on, but she couldn't quite put her finger on what. I was really acting strange. I lost 40 pounds in two months. I wasn't eating food. I was just grumpy and nodding out all the time. She knew something was going on.

I had a friend, Maddy, at the time. She was almost 70 years old. She was cool. She liked to smoke pot, and she was funny. I met her when we bred our dog with her stud. Her husband, Bob, was a Vietnam veteran, a jet pilot who was shot down over Northern Vietnam. I really liked these people. I paid their taxes once so they didn't lose their house. It cost me $6,000. She'd come over to visit and I'd ask her about Bob. "Oh, he's home on the couch. He can't move. He's in pain."

I'd give her handfuls of pills. "Here. Take these home and give 'em to Bob. Take 'em. Whatever you gotta do to help Bob out."

One day they put Maddy on some fucked up meds, and she had this moment of truth. She decided to call my girlfriend

Ronda and tell her, "Hey, by the way, you know the other day when I was over? Alton was out there snorting pills."

I was caught. Ronda almost left me. I almost lost everything. I almost lost my home. I almost lost what I had for family now. I almost lost myself. That was a bad time.

I finally started to see that maybe this life, these drugs aren't so great. Maybe this isn't the best idea. I decided I wasn't chasing this shit anymore. I have something here that means something. What I have is way too important to lose over some goddamn painkillers. I had to open my eyes.

I've tried to pull myself off drugs many times before. I've spent days and weeks in my mother's living room detoxing. I shook and shit myself and puked all over the place. I couldn't even get up. I had a temperature of almost 105. I was shaking and sweating. I was cold, but I couldn't stand to have a blanket over me. It was bad, but it never opened my eyes to reality. I would just tell myself, "I'm not going to do that drug anymore," and I'd move onto something different. It never worked. Every drug feels the same coming off it. Detox is detox no matter if it's heroin, cocaine, opiates, or pills. It all feels the same. It feels like shit. When I went to jail, I never stopped anything. I picked it right back up where I left off soon as I got out.

This time it was different. This life with Ronda and our family – that was my eye opener. I finally came to a realization: if anything in this life is important to me, I want to fucking smarten up now.

I didn't go chasing pills anymore. I started canceling

people out of my life that used to be really good friends of mine because they still did drugs. I didn't need that around me. I didn't want it. If it's around me, that possibility is always there – I might slip. I really have to be on my toes and watch what I'm doing, where I am, and who I'm with. I have to really be in touch with how I feel every day. The days that I'm really down and out, those are the days thoughts creep in. *Wouldn't it be great just to escape? Just to get away and not bother with this. Not have to think about it. Not have to deal with it.* It was really crazy for me.

That was the biggest turning point in my life, just the realization that I had been caught. I had to actually be honest with her. I asked myself, "What are you going to do here?"

I think that's when I realized what Ronda was actually going through. She should have walked out the door a long time ago. The first time I threw a vodka bottle across the room and it bounced off the wall and hit her, she should have walked out. She's been through some shit with me. She's put up with me crashing the house, breaking the table, throwing liquor bottles all over the place at people. She should have said to me, "You're a putz," long ago and moved on. But she didn't. She stuck in there. I can't begin to tell you why. I was always into myself more than anything. She stuck by me. For a little while she held it against me. But now, she doesn't. No matter what, she's got my back. She's there for me. My step children helped me through it too. They told me I was a good person and they loved me. It was really helpful for me to be able to hear that. If they only knew how much that meant to me. I love them so much and am forever grateful for their love and support.

I don't think I would have wanted to turn that corner in my life without Ronda. I wouldn't have bothered. I'd be out looking for my next high. I'd probably have overdosed by now because I was doing 30 pills a day. I mean that's a big habit, especially when they're 15, thirty-milligram pills. Without that relationship to ground me, I'd probably be dead.

So, I wasn't dead. But I didn't know where to go from there. I didn't see the point. Not yet.

The Nuttiest Woman I've Ever Met

I was in limbo, just floating aimlessly through my life for the next few years after I finally got off the drugs. I had a lot inside, and I never told anyone what was going on. I didn't even know what was going on inside me. All I knew was that there was a pile of shit in there. I was getting depressed a lot. Sometimes I wouldn't want to get out of bed for a week. I wouldn't take a shower. I wouldn't shave. *Just fuck everybody. I don't care anymore.* Then a week later I'd feel happy, or I'd think I was happy.

My license had been suspended long ago, and I wasn't supposed to be driving. One day Ronda was sick, I couldn't get hold of my sister, and my neighbor was drunk, so I drove a mile down the road to buy dinner and some medicine. Of course, I got pulled over and they gave me another driving charge.

Instead of going to jail again I went to the Reentry program in Belfast for six months. It's a program for men coming out of prison. They try to teach life skills and how to communicate with your family.

I thought, "This is stupid. They've piled me up with classes – 300 hours of this shit. None of these classes even make sense. Resilience class. Epictetus Club. Mindfulness class. Meditation. They're all stupid. I should have just done my time in jail. How does this even pertain to my life?"

I went to this Nonviolent Communication class (NVC) taught by a woman named Peggy Smith. In the first class I told her she was crazy. I said, "You're the nuttiest woman I've ever met. You're higher than I've ever been if you think I'm going to sit here in this class with a bunch of men and talk to you about how I feel. You're nuts. It's not happening. Let's just forget this."

During my second Nonviolent Communication class, Peggy asked us to tell a story about a time we did something nice for someone. I told her, "I ain't never done nothin' nice for anybody." Then I thought about it. A memory surfaced.

One time Ronda and I saw this Christmas tree with a bunch of papers on it at Wal-Mart in Bangor. I thought this is a weird way to decorate a tree. I looked closer and saw each piece of paper had a child's name on it, their age, and what they wanted for Christmas. These kids had nothing.

My father had died earlier that year of mesothelioma from working with asbestos. My siblings and I won a lawsuit, so I was walking around Wal-Mart with a pocket of $100 bills that would scare you. I didn't see anybody else buying anything for these Christmas tree children. What else are you going to do when you have $40,000 in the bank?

Right then and there, I emptied the tree. We ended up spending a LOT of money. I bought portable DVD players, helmets, kneepads, and skateboards. I had two carts. Ronda had two carts.

When we pulled up to the checkout, I asked the woman behind the counter, "Now where do you want all this stuff?"

She says, "Sir, I don't understand."

I said, "Do you see any papers on your tree? Your tree's gone."

"Are you serious?"

"I'm pretty serious. Now, where do you want this stuff? I want to go back. I still have to get bicycles. And I want to go home tonight, so let's get this shit moving."

"Oh my God. Just push 'em over there."

"By the way, I'm going to need some help, because I'm going to need almost every bicycle you got on your rack." So we went back and got bicycles. It was crazy. It was quite a night.

I shared that story in class. Peggy asked me, "Now that you remember that, how do you feel?" I didn't know how to even think about that question. I was so high when it happened; I'm lucky I even thought to look at the tree. I never considered how I felt.

I went back to my bunk and thought about it and cried. *Wow. Maybe I have done something good for people.* I felt good, really good. I had never been able to pick out good feelings. I didn't know what it meant. It wasn't my usual feelings of rage.

I know what it's like to not have anything. When I was a

kid we didn't have shit. We'd buy sneakers from the Salvation Army that already had holes in them. I was lucky to get four pairs of socks at Christmas. My mom wrapped two pairs in each package so it looked like I was getting two presents. I know they did the best they could. We didn't have a lot, but we always had something to eat.

When I finally connected the feeling, that came from remembering that act of kindness at Wal-Mart, to the needs inside me, needs I didn't really know I had, this class took on a whole new meaning. It showed me that everything I had done in life was driven by my needs. It was so true. It was so true. I thought, *She's not crazy anymore. This woman knows what she's talking about.*

ABC's of Inner Boxing

When I was in prison I took a lot of the same kind of classes I was taking at the Reentry Center. Each time, I thought, *Boy, I learned a lot.* Actually, I didn't absorb anything. I didn't give it a chance. Nothing ever changed. I just went back to the same old drugs, same old thought patterns, and same old self-hate. But this time, something was different. The lessons seemed to actually pertain to my real life. Something clicked. It wasn't just talk.

At the Reentry Center, in The Epictetus Club we learned about the ABCs of inner boxing. A is the attacking thought such *as I'm going to fucking beat your head.* B is the blocking thought. *What do I want to happen here? How is this going to affect me? How is this going to affect others?* C is the counter punch. *Well, let's not do this. I can walk away from this. It doesn't have to happen.* This idea resonated with me because I needed to hear that. I never felt like I had any control in these kinds of situations. It always seemed like my mind left me and my fists took over. I began to understand my motivations, my reasons for attacking. The reasons are within me, not the situation. I began to breed Epictetus and Nonviolent Communication together, creating a whole new baby – Altonphant.

I also began to excel in my Nonviolent Communication class. One of the first things we learned was to observe our feelings and connect them with our needs. I now often stop and do a self-inventory. *How am I feeling in this moment? What do I need out of this situation?* For example, I might be sitting in a room full of angry people and I'll notice I'm triggered by it. I'll ask myself, how am I feeling? If I notice I feel uncomfortable or nervous I can connect it to what I need. I might have a need for calmness or safety. If I can keep in touch with my feelings I can choose my reaction. I know I don't have to get involved in an argument or fight. I can sit back on the sidelines and not be a part of it. Or, if I feel confident that I can de-escalate the situation, I might say, "Hey, is this really what you guys want to do?" Instead of feeding off their anger – I feel it, I understand it, and I choose my response.

This process was so foreign to me at first, but it was also a huge relief. I didn't like talking about my feelings. That was baby stuff, girlie stuff. The way I was raised, men don't talk about their feelings. But I could see that my feelings came from somewhere: from my needs. My life started to make more sense.

By the time I was released from the Reentry program I felt I had better tools to handle my life. Little did I know, I had gotten the attention of the trainer, Peggy Smith. She looked up my information and called me. "I have never done this before," she said, "so I'm just gonna jump to it." Then she asked me if I would like to help her co-teach the class.

"Wow." I said, "You realize who this is right?"

"Yeah. Alton, right?"

I almost told her I wouldn't do it. For most of my life, if I thought I might fail, I wouldn't even bother trying. I don't like failure, and I don't like looking stupid. That's been a big thing for me. But I said, yes. Here I am, over a year later, I'm still going at it. I'm still teaching this class.

Curious Compassion

At the first class I taught at the Reentry Center, I started by introducing myself. I gave the guys a look into my background. I told them about the things that happened to me: sexual abuse, violence, drug problems, the disconnect with my father. These were stories that for a long time I didn't tell anybody. Once I did that, I saw that nobody laughed at me, nobody said, "You're a fuckin' idiot. Shut up." Instead these men thanked me. I was taken aback. "Thank you for that? What do you mean?" Around the circle, the men took turns telling me how much of an inspiration hearing my story was for them. After that I started telling more people my story.

Something amazing happens when I do this. I can see how revealing my story, my emotions, even just my presence, is already helping people. It's helping the men at the Reentry Center to be comfortable within themselves. I've found that a lot of our stories overlap. We have a connection. A lot of the guys will say, "Wow that happened to me too, but I never dared to say that." I've had conversations with some of the toughest guys in this town, guys I've known since I was 12 years old who are tougher than nails. They come from the same background. Some have experienced molestation and violence. Some have grown up in families with no connection, no love, many feel alone. It's crazy how closely our stories overlap. Knowing that gives me the courage I need to keep telling my story.

When I first started opening up and talking about my experience with sexual abuse I would tell my story in all its brutality. I would spit this shit out. People would react like,

"Oh my God. Why'd you tell me that? I realize that happened to you, but why would you talk like that?" I guess when I first started talking about it I was still angry. I'm not angry anymore. At some level I've come to accept what happened. I've somehow forgiven the man who molested me.

About five years ago I went into the convenience store where he works. I walked up to the counter and boom; I was face to face with him. I was growling. He just put his head down. I said, "Give me my shit back. Fuck you, dude." I went down to the other cashier. I stopped going in that store for years. For years I dreamed about how I was gonna kill him, how I was gonna tie him to a chair and cut his fucking head off. That's what I dreamed of at night. Now I think about it, and I have this sadness for him.

I've gone back into the store a few times recently, because now it doesn't bother me. I've come to acceptance. I wonder how he was feeling when that happened. Maybe something bad happened to him; you never know. Maybe he had no way to express it. Maybe he lacked the tools to accept himself. I don't really know what happened to him, but I am curious. That little bit of curiosity gives me the compassion to say, "It's all right, man. Everybody makes a mistake." For me to be able to come to this curiosity and forgiveness is the biggest step I've ever made in my life. I don't want to see this person hurt.

I've taken my power back and then some. For so many years I gave my power to other people. It's great to be able to have my own power, to be able to control my own actions, to control my own destiny. It's like the sky's the limit. Now I'm able to look at people with love. I look at life as something we should cherish. No matter what people do, everybody matters. If we didn't have each other, what would we have? Somehow we're all connected. We're all humans. No matter what we do in our lives.

The Convict Becomes
The Teacher

In prison, it's about survival. If you hold eye contact with somebody in prison too long, it's a fight. If you sit in somebody's seat at the dinner table, you're lucky you don't get a tray wrapped around your head. You don't touch my stuff. You don't come in my room. You don't do this and you don't do that. You keep your head down. You shut your mouth. You don't see nothing. You don't hear nothing. You don't say nothing. You have to lock yourself within yourself for protection, for safety.

Many of the men at the Reentry Center have been indoctrinated by the prison culture before they arrive. That is the world they know and understand. After they've been in the Reentry Center for a little while though, I've noticed a switch in their attitudes and how they treat each other. It's pretty awesome for them to be able to come from a culture that's so closed off to a place where it's totally open. You don't have to worry if you look at me for five seconds. If you want to sit in my seat, please do. It's such a different lifestyle for them. A lot of guys are in shock when they come in. But the guys that are in shock — I think these are the first guys to really take a hard look at NVC because it gives them a sense of freedom. Now they treat each other like they're in a community. They're concerned for each other. If they see one guy that's down in the dumps, a couple guys will come and ask, "Hey, how you doin'? What can we do for ya?" They try to help each other. It's beautiful to see that.

When I first started teaching, I'd start talking and I'd have tears running out of me. I couldn't stop it. These guys are looking at me like, "Wow. What's wrong with this guy?" I didn't stop. I kept crying. It didn't matter anymore who's watching. A lot of these men have never had another man sit in front of them in that kind of an emotional state and be willing to show it. So it gives them a little bit of inspiration to connect with their own lives. The guys are really receptive to my presence and my stories. They see I've been on their side of the table most of my life. I'm normally the one locked up, taking these classes, listening to somebody babble on in the front of the room.

It gives me a certain credibility when they find out that I've been in prison for attempted murder and aggravated assault. They look at me and they say, "Wow, and you're here to teach us?" It's kind of insane to think these guys look up to me like a role model. "You've made it. You've done this. You've been out of this hole. How'd you do it? I want to be like you."

I never heard anybody tell me that before. Nobody ever wanted to be like me. I didn't even want to be like me. I'm really growing and developing a lot of beautiful relationships with people.

I get enjoyment out of connecting with other people and having conversations, even in the grocery store. I'll go in the grocery store and my girlfriend will get upset sometimes because I take forever. Sometimes I'll talk to three or four different people in the store just trying to get a jug of milk. I never found that to be enjoyable before. I didn't want to hear what other people had to say. Three or four years ago I would never have said that I wanted a relationship like that with other people. I wanted other people to just leave me alone. You don't know me. You don't know what I've been through, so just back off. But now I've found that by talking to people I learn a lot, and really I like it.

I like to help other people find this inner peace within themselves. It brings a sense of happiness and fulfillment to my life. I just really enjoy being helpful. It may sound funny, but it's my contribution to life. Maybe it's my way to make up for some of the heinous acts I've committed. I'm grateful for every chance because I get to see how I have purpose in life. To go through life without any sense of purpose, it's a pretty dull, lonely life. Today I don't feel lonely. There are 50 different people I can connect with at any given moment whether it's by email, a phone call, "Hey want to meet for coffee? Want to have lunch?" That's my support system. It makes me feel good to reach out and say, "Hey, how ya doin'? Is there anything I can do for you? What would you like of me?" It's awesome. It might seem simple, but it's really huge. Hopefully others can catch on to that.

I know you can't change the world overnight. Change happens one small piece at a time. Eventually you'll notice it. When it becomes noticeable, that means you've done what you set out to do and you know you're succeeding. This is what gives me the drive to keep going.

The Pause

One morning I walked into the Reentry Center to teach a group of men with Peggy. I walked in and I saw the guy who was dating my sister. His face turned colors. I went up to him and said, "What's going on?"

He said, "Apparently you've heard."

I said, 'Heard what?"

"I'm in here for aggravated assault on your sister."

Three years ago, if this guy would have said this to me, I would have tipped him out of his chair and beat him with it. I wouldn't have stopped beating him with his chair until he couldn't move.

I said to him, "Shit gets crazy sometimes," and I walked away. I was there to teach a class, my true intention for being there. I've never been able to walk away from a confrontation like that before.

Between the time he told me and my response I took a deep breath and became aware that I felt furious. I was really angry, sad, and hurt. I felt depressed. I connected those feelings with the needs I have for the things I value. I value order, support, and integrity. I want to be seen for who I am, to be seen for my true intentions.

When I looked at my feelings and needs I'd already begun

to nourish my needs. I didn't have to react with violence. I didn't have to beat him with his chair, because I knew what my needs were. My reaction is totally within myself now. That's choice. I never knew I had the choice before. My reaction was always, bang! Let's fight. Now I have the choice.

I even went home that night and paced the floor thinking somehow I had done an injustice to my sister because I didn't react and honor her. All I could think of was what my father would have said to me if he were alive, "You're a fucking pansy not defending your sister!"

But I was there for her in a totally calm way. I called her up and I told her, "If there's anything I can do, I'm here." She was amazed.

I realized she let me walk into this situation. She knew I worked there and that I would see him. Both of my sisters knew this and let me walk into it. I was angry with them. I called my other sister the day after I had a chance to think about it. I try to give myself 24 hours before I get into something that bothers me a lot. She said, "Well Alton, we know how you react to things like this. We didn't want to lose our brother." Wow. That sat me down. It made me think. I couldn't be mad at them. I had a better understanding of why they didn't tell me, because I have always responded in a bad way. But after hearing the words from my sisters that they're very proud of me and grateful for me, I thought, *Wow. I've never heard that before. I've never heard that from any of my family, let alone my sisters.* It was really a celebration. I felt more love for myself and the possibility that I could be there for others in the same kind of genuine way. It gave me that drive to learn more, to really try to put NVC to use even more.

If I had gone with my gut reaction and beat that man till he couldn't move, it would be like throwing everything that I'd been trying to learn and teach about nonviolent communication out the window. I'd be a hypocrite. How could I react like that? Well, it's about the pause.

They say true freedom is the ability to pause between the stimulus and the response.[3] It's so true. I have my own freedom. I could choose how I reacted to this situation. I don't have to react on impulse. I had the choice. That's so huge for me. It's a totally different thought process.

Violence starts at the base of thought. Violence isn't just external. There is internal violence against your own spirit. I've had that for a long time, and I didn't even realize that it was violence. I thought it was just something that happened. That's the kind of stuff we try to teach. My inside violence causes my exterior violence. When I get pissed off at myself, when I judge myself, I want to hurt somebody. It goes hand in hand for me.

Today stuff comes at me and I can choose how I respond. I hear news about how a loved one tried to commit suicide. My sister was strangled by her boyfriend. My niece was beat up by a guy that used to be in the Reentry Center. All these things could have triggered a psychotic rage. I work through it. Yes, I still feel bad. I still get angry, but I can recognize that now. I recognize when I feel angry that it's something inside of me. It's not that person making me angry. Other people don't have

---

3   This saying is often attributed to both Viktor Frankl (www. viktorfrankl.org) and psychologist Rollo May.

that power to create my emotions. Only I can do that. It took me a long time to realize that. Every time I was mad it had to be somebody else that made me mad, so I'd hurt them. I can look at day-to-day life and face it. I can work through it. I can still feel like I have some self-worth, like I have some sort of purpose. I never would have guessed. I don't think anybody in my family would ever have guessed. It's really changed my life, showed me a new way.

I look at life on a continuum. On one end of this continuum you have war, genocide, extreme violence. On the other end you have genuine connection and authenticity. Human beings are the most savage species I've ever seen in my life. Some of the things that we can do to each other with a smile on our face – I can't even read the newspaper anymore. Mothers hurting their babies, punching their kids in the face. Kids stabbing their parents to death. It makes me sick. It makes me wonder, what went so wrong? Is there any help for us? Everybody has the capacity for violence. I know my capacity for violence is still here. I could snap at any moment. But I also carry the knowledge that I have choice. Choice is very powerful. I can choose not to react like that. So, everybody has the capacity for either. We each have the capacity for violence and the capacity for goodness, for kindness. In between this continuum, everybody has the capacity for change.

Looking Stupid

I don't like looking stupid, and I don't like failing. I've done a lot of stupid things trying to avoid looking stupid. It's a fear I'm learning to face. After I got out of prison, I thought I was ready to face that fear and make a change in my life. I thought I was ready to grab life by the horns. My sisters really encouraged me to attend college, particularly Laurie. She said, "I'll go with you. We'll take the same class. I'll help you. I want to see you do good."

It was really easy for me to get my GED. I went in and took the pre-test and scored over 700. I didn't even study. The only problem was math. I thought maybe I was a little smarter than I am. I thought I could do college the same way I did the test. It was through the University of Maine in Augusta, but I took my classes at the Hutchinson Center in Belfast.

For some crazy reason I picked the major with the most math in it. I was going for a bachelor's degree in architecture. I really set myself up off the bat for failure. I quit math in sixth grade. I can't even do long division. My first math class in college was overwhelming. I had never even seen algebra before. I could do the math in my head, but I couldn't write it out on paper. The teacher kept writing notes on my work, "The answers are great. You need to show the work. That cuts half of your grade off when you can't show the work." I kept writing on the paper. "I can't do the work on paper. I can do it in my head, and I can give you the right answer."

I started repeating the same kind of behavior I had as a

child in school. I wouldn't raise my hand to ask a question because I didn't want to look like the stupid kid. Even today I have a hard time looking like the stupid person. If I see that I might fail at something, a lot of times I won't even try it. When I fail I really kick the shit out of myself. That's the way I've always been.

In between taking math and world government classes I rewarded myself with a good high. Every time I finished a paper and thought I did it right, I'd get high. The information wasn't sinking in. Getting high in between really wasn't the answer.

One day I went to my math class, and we were having a test. Of course I got stoned first thing that morning. On the second to last page of the test there were six questions on the back. I didn't realize it, never even looked at the back of the page. I failed. I needed a C+. I got a C. If I had realized those six questions were there, I probably would have passed my math class.

I told myself, I'm not cut out for this. I'm not smart enough for all this stuff. I just failed the most important class for this major. So, what's the sense? So I dropped out. I figured getting high was better than looking stupid. Like a lot of things in my life, I gave up on the dream of it.

This past year I had another chance to face my fear of failure. Peggy and I taught a NVC class to the staff at Riverview Psychiatric Hospital. I gave a 30-minute lecture at the beginning of every class. I told them everything, from being molested as a kid, to having shit for relationships with my kids, and the resentments that followed. I didn't hold back. It really caught their attention. The staff started talking about how maybe I could help their hospital; help make it a safer place, a happier work environment. The year before many of the staff were assaulted by clients and some were still not back to work. This is the stuff they wanted to change. They thought, with my knowledge of the dynamics of violence and my background of being engaged in a lot of violence, I had something to offer. A bunch of the staff told the superintendent, "You gotta check this guy out. This guy is the breath of fresh air we need in here. He has the life experience. He can read people. He can look and tell you if this person is ready for violence or what their mental state is just by talking to them." I have a knack for that now.

He asked me to apply for a job at the hospital, as an Acuity Specialist. It's a new position they created to take over for the correction staff. I said to him, "I'm a felon. I have attempted murder on my record. I have aggravated assaults." I said, "Do you realize that?"

He could see the strength I have connecting with people. He could see my potential. He told me, "You push through with the interview. You let me worry about the felonies." I brought him a list of all my felonies. I went to the court and had them print them off for me. He said it wasn't that bad. It's kind of weird. All this stuff that I've been hiding from for all these years, thinking, Well, I can't do that because I'm a felon, maybe it's not as bad as I think.

I've never been offered anything like this opportunity, ever. This is a $44,000/year position, plus all the benefits. I've never had anything like that. Applying for this job scared me. Like I said, I don't like looking stupid, and I don't like failing. This is a position you're supposed to have four years of college before you can even put in an application. I didn't get past the first semester of college. I do, however, have the knowledge and the tools and the strength to do this job well. But, it's still hard for me to let go of my fear of letting everybody down, of letting myself down . . . like I've always done. A lot of people have faith in me, and I don't want to prove them wrong.

This time I decided I'm not going to run away from it just because I'm scared. I can admit that I'm scared. When I was in college I couldn't admit I was afraid. Today, I can actually go into the office for the interview and say, "Look guys, I'm scared shitless. I'm really scared. I'm really nervous. Please bear with me." And it just seems to work itself out. Things just come together. All I had to do was be myself. I had to be authentic. It's okay to be a little scared. It just keeps you on your game. It's gonna drive me to do my best, to make sure that I'm responsible, that I'm professional.

I never would have said I had anything to offer anybody. I never would have said, "Let me be a role model for you." That's not even close to sounding right. Role model? No, you don't want to follow me. That's the worst thing you can do. No, you don't want to follow me at all. But, now I do have a lot of people that follow my example. Sometimes it's really baffling to me that people have so much faith in me. I don't really feel like I've ever done anything to gain that kind of faith really. They think I've done a lot. I feel like I'm just scratching the surface.

It's about getting past that scared part. Not giving up. Resilience. You've got to persevere. You've got to push through this – even if you do look stupid, big deal. That's the way I had to look at it. I've since found out that I did not get the job. There were a few charges on my record they couldn't work around. Yet, I am honored they asked me to apply, they thought so highly of me they could see my past as a positive aspect of my knowledge and experience. They have shown me hope.

To me, it's amazing. The big thing was getting over that fear of failure. I can fail. It doesn't make me look stupid. What matters is to keep your head up and push on.

Crying in Public

"I hate you."

"I never want to see you again."

"If you ever come near me again I'm going to bash you in the face."

The last time I spoke with my son, these were our parting words. My son went on to tell people he wanted to grow up to kill his father. It was really crazy. Then he saw me on TV four years later. I did a news interview for the Reentry Center as one of their success stories. Alton was watching the news and saw me. He asked his foster parents if he could visit with me. He actually wanted a visit. At first I was really scared at the idea of seeing my son again. I almost said no. I almost called him and said I couldn't do it.

We met at the co-op and sat down in the cafe. I was nervous. I hadn't seen him or talked to him in almost four years. I didn't know what to say. I was shaking. Right away I was authentic with him. I just started off telling him how I felt. I figured it would be good to get that out. "I'm really kind of scared of this situation. Makes me nervous. I'm anxious." I expressed how hurt I was by my actions, how I treated him and his sister.

Within five minutes I had tears running out of me like a little baby. I was crying. I was actually displaying emotions in public with 30 people nearby to look on. I mean the place was full. We were lucky to get a table. My son looked at me like I had two heads. "Oh my god, what are you doing man?" He looked around at the other people to see their reactions to my tears.

I told him, "I'm human, man. Humans do this stuff. If I continue to not show emotion, Alton, I wouldn't be a human. It's totally okay. You know, I've cried in this place more times than you've picked your nose. Most of these people would come and ask if they could give you a hug and see if you're doing all right. Honestly, that's how people are Alton. People aren't vicious like we portray them to be."

As I spoke, I realized something: "The only me you've ever known was a father with no feelings, that would not display emotions. If you came to me and said, 'I love you,' I gave you the same answer my father gave me: 'Yep.' I never said, 'I love you too, son,' or 'Good job,' or 'I'm proud of you.' There was none of that. Usually it was, 'Get out of my face.'"

After a few minutes, we were crying together. He saw that it was okay to express emotions, even in public. We cried together. We apologized. Automatic connection. I came to him in a way that he could accept. They say for true dialogue, both sides have to be willing to change. What we had was true dialogue.

It was a beautiful moment. As soon as I started talking, I felt this connection like I've never had with the kid, like we were both there wholly for each other. We were probably there for two hours. When we were done he gave me a hug and a kiss and told me he loves me. You know what? He'd like to have another visit.

His foster mother texted me when he got home. She told me Alton talked the whole way home in the car about how amazed he was by the changes in me. He's had a lot of the same problems I've had in life. We don't express feelings of weakness, like fear or feeling hurt. On his bad days, he thinks about some of the stuff he's been through, and he becomes destructive to himself. After that visit he had another bad day, but instead of hurting himself he went to his foster mother and said, "Can I talk to you?" She said, "Sure." He actually communicated how he felt. He told her, "I don't want hurt myself anymore." So he actually communicated to her his feelings and his need for physical safety and integrity.

A couple of years ago, if you would have told me that this would have happened I would have laughed at you. I would have told you, "I never wanna see those kids again in my life." Really, I wasn't angry with my kids. I was angry with myself. I didn't know how to be a parent. I didn't know how to express my feelings or connect or communicate with other people. It's such a big change to come from the hatred and the despising. So I'm glad to hear my son's voice now. He tells me how he feels and what's going on. He's communicating feelings. I'd never thought I'd see that. I guess things are moving in a good direction.

Self-Empathy

I was digging really deep inside of myself after my visit with my son. There was something bothering me, and I couldn't put a finger on it. It was eating at me. I practiced self-empathy and I really delved into myself, just really listened to myself. I figured out a lot. I found that everything in my life that I cried for, all the attention from my parents, hoping to hear, "I love you," the recognition that I dreamed of that I never got, I took that away from my kids too.

I know that I've always loved my kids. But I showed that love in a hard way. It was always "Shut your mouth. I don't want to hear you crying. You're not a baby. Get out of my face man. I got stuff to do." If they spoke up about their feelings I told my kids, "You fuckin' people think your life's so bad? Let me tell you a little bit about life." I never thought they deserved a voice about it, because, to me, their life didn't seem that bad. They probably wanted a dad to say, "I love you," a dad to be there as a dad. I was too blind to see that. I couldn't let myself see that. I pushed them away. I pushed them out of my life. Why? Because of my own fears inside of me? It doesn't make sense to me anymore.

This experience made me realize what I have to do. I need to put my old hatred away. I need to accept it, I need to understand it, and I need to put it into perspective. It's not their fault. I don't think they woke up every morning saying, "Let's be a shit to Dad." They were probably confused, asking the same questions I was asking. "How could you do that?"

Somewhere in all of this, of course, I also have to forgive my parents. They too grew up in a culture of violence. They did the best they could. My father's father would smack you in the face with a wrench if you pissed him off. He really didn't care. His father was even worse. Violence. Angry, angry, explosive people. My father had to take what he learned. He was a good man in some ways. He made sure the family was provided for. He worked every day of the week. He worked in the rain, he worked in the snow. He started work before the sun rose and stopped late after dark. No, we didn't have a father that was around all the time, and we didn't have any nice things, but we had something to eat, we had a place to live, even if our sneakers came from the Salvation Army with holes already in them.

Once I saw that connection between my relationship with my father and my relationship with my kids, it felt horrible. It hurt a lot to uncover this. But it also gave me an inspiration to be there for my kids. Try to show them I'm sorry. I want to be part of their lives like I've never been before. Every time I see my son now, I give him a big hug and say, "I love you. I can't wait to see you again." Is that so hard? Is that too much for a kid to ask for? Doesn't seem so. But that's something that I had to accept. I had to accept that I did that to my kids. In a way, they grew up without a father, without that role model in their life. I can't change that. I can't go back and redo this. I had to mourn that fact. I had to accept it, and I had to move on. I'm going to fix this by what I do from here on, what I do in the rest of my life.

Since that first visit with Alton, we've met every week. We've had dinner and gone bowling. I hope I have a chance to get closer to both of my kids. We're talking about going fishing. I'm actually looking forward to it. Before I really wouldn't look forward to something like that. It would seem like a burden. Now I want to do this. It has been a big difference in my attitude and my outlook toward my children and my life. They're a part of me.

It's kind of mind boggling. Talking about your feelings and needs. Communicating with love and compassion. It seems so simple. Why hasn't everybody tried this? But it's hard work getting there. I shed a lot of tears over this process. It's not easy. I had to open up wounds inside of me that I've tried to forget. I couldn't just scratch them a little bit. I had to really tear them open. And I did. I got through it – and it was such a relief, a feeling of, "Wow. I held that against myself for so long. Why?" Everybody makes mistakes. It was those tragic expressions of my needs. I didn't know what else to do. I had no other tools. I had no other way. But once you open those wounds and start healing there is a sense of wholeness. Wow, I have the whole me. I have the me that I don't mind. I actually don't mind being in the same room with myself. I never wanted to be alone because I hated myself. I've come so far from that. Now I want to spend time with me, with other people, with my kids. For my children to be able to see this in me, it hits home to me how this process can work, how it can help.

Hope

I have a lot of hopes. I hope for peace. I hope that I can keep doing this. I hope that I can keep helping others. I hope that I can continue to enjoy helping and connecting with people. I hope that I can keep compassion in my life because I know somewhere deep down if I wake up in the morning and have no compassion, I'm done. I'm right back to where I was before. I hope that in every situation I walk into I can maintain and stay true to myself. I guess that's my big hope. My hope is for happiness, for peace, for love. I hope for health and well-being. I hope my kids and I can develop a stronger relationship than we ever would've had.

I hope for change. That some day maybe there could be a little more peace in the world due to some of the stuff we teach. I hope every person I talk to, every person that we have in class, I hope they go back out into the world and try to make something for themselves, that they try to put some of this stuff to use and connect with their families and the people that they love. I hope that their families accept them for who they are and learn to say, "Well, stuff happens. I know you've done this, but I love you anyway." I hope others can have the same feelings of inner peace and love that I have, that I've just recently acquired.

THE END ....

Or The Next Beginning

Resources

Alton refers to two processes that greatly supported his inner transformation. Here are sources to find out more.

"The Epictetus Club: Lessons from the Walls" by Jeff Traylor http://epictetusclub.com

Nonviolent Communication is a process developed by Marshall Rosenberg, PhD. To learn more about this process and world-wide resources: www.cnvc.org

To connect to Alton Lane & his NVC mentor Peggy Smith: http://www.opencommunication.org

Also on that site is the curriculum that they use at the Reentry Center, entitled "Courageous Communication". This document posted as a free downloadable pdf

http://opencommunication.org/resources.html

http://altonlane-onlyhuman.com

Acknowledgements & Gratitude

First of all I would like to say that this is a memoir of life through my eyes and my eyes alone. Any disagreement – I'm sorry.

This book is dedicated to my beautiful family.

Mom and Dad, I will love and miss you forever. Thank you for being you and always doing the best you could for us. I love you!

Ronda, you are my heart. I love you so much! You have been beside me through some horrible times in my life. I don't know what I would do without you. When I felt I didn't have the strength to fight my opiate addiction – I looked to you and got the strength. I needed to change my life and you were my rock. Thank you for everything you do for me. I love you.

Brittany, Blaine and Taylor, my oldest children. I am truly grateful to have you in my life. You have helped me to understand and experience what it means to unconditionally love another person. You never gave up on me, no matter what. You believed in me when I didn't believe in myself. Thank you so much for the joy you bring to my life. I will love you and be there for you. There will always be a special place in my heart for each of you. I am very proud of the young adults you have become. I love you to the moon and back!

Sharon and Alton, my birth children, I love and miss you both so much. I often find myself asking, "Where did things go so wrong?" I am sorry for a lot of the decisions I have made in my life and so wish that someday we can let go of the past and start to build a new relationship with love and understanding. You are a part of me and I hope to someday have the chance to be the dad I never was, to prove to you that I truly do love you with all my heart. Please forgive me for my mistakes in life and meet the real me. I will always be here when and if you are ready.

My beautiful granddaughter McKinley, thank you for the smiles you bring to us and for helping me to see how beautiful and precious life really is. You are perfect and I look forward to many years of watching you learn and grow. I love you and am truly thankful to have you in my life.

My sisters, thank you for being you. You inspire me to better my life and help others also. I love you more than words can say.

And, My Ma, you have been a part of my life for a long time and you have always accepted me and encouraged me to be myself no matter what. I know you have my back and truly cherish our relationship. Thank you for being there for me. I love you.

Finally, this book would never have come to be without the skill and care of two people. Meghan, I appreciate your skill in crafting questions, listening and bringing order and flow to the story of my life. Your care and heart brought this manuscript to life. Howard, your generosity and skill turned the manuscript into a book. Thank you both for all your efforts.

Made in the USA
Middletown, DE
28 May 2019